# Twisted Faith:
# Christian Zionism

Exposing Christian Zionism's War on

**Palestine** and **Humanity**

**Bilal Shammout**

# Table of Contents

# Preface: A Word on Faith, Respect, and Clarity

I did not write this book as a theologian. I am not one, and I do not wish to be understood as critiquing theology. That is a task for theologians, and many have already done so with great depth and courage. My purpose is different: to share a personal journey and a moral confrontation.

This book is a reflection of my personal journey, an attempt to make sense of experiences I could not explain at the time. It is a reckoning with the silence I encountered, the empathy that vanished, and the theology that seemed to justify suffering. It is not an academic exercise. It is a moral confrontation.

*Twisted Faith: Christian Zionism* is not a critique of Christianity, Judaism, or any sacred tradition. It is a focused examination of a specific theological-political ideology, Christian Zionism, and its profound impact on global politics, religious discourse, and, most urgently, the Palestinian people.

Christian Zionism is not synonymous with Christianity. It is a modern movement, primarily rooted in evangelical Protestantism, that interprets biblical prophecy as a mandate to support the modern state of Israel, often unconditionally and at the expense of Palestinian rights. This book challenges that ideology, not the faith of millions who follow Christ's teachings of love, justice, and compassion.

I recognize that some readers, especially within Arab Christian communities, may feel discomfort at the association of Christianity with Zionism. That discomfort is valid. But let me be clear: this book does not conflate Christianity with Christian Zionism. On the contrary, it seeks to draw a sharp distinction between the two. While Christianity teaches love for neighbor, humility, and care for the oppressed, Christian Zionism often promotes division, supremacy, and apocalyptic confrontation.

Many Christians, Arab and otherwise, have stood in courageous solidarity with Palestine. Their voices are honored and amplified here. This book is a call to reclaim the moral core of faith from those who have distorted it into a tool of empire and exclusion.

## What, then, is Christian Zionism?

It is a theological-political movement that views the modern state of Israel as the fulfillment of biblical prophecy and therefore deserving of unwavering political, financial, and theological support. This belief is not metaphorical, it is literal. It shapes how millions of Christians interpret scripture, foreign policy, and the Israeli–Palestinian conflict.

Scholars have defined it in various ways:

### Stephen Sizer (2004):
"A movement within Protestant evangelicalism that sees the modern state of Israel as the fulfillment of biblical prophecy and thus deserving of political, financial, and theological support."

**Yaakov Ariel (2013):**

"A belief system that combines Christian eschatology with political activism, viewing the return of Jews to the Holy Land as a necessary step toward the Second Coming of Christ."

**Donald Wagner (1995):**

"A political movement within Protestant fundamentalism that seeks to influence U.S. foreign policy in support of Israel, based on a literalist reading of biblical prophecy."

**Robert Owen Smith (2013):**

"Political action, guided by specific Christian commitments, aimed at promoting or preserving Jewish control over the geographic area now containing Israel and the occupied Palestinian territories."

These definitions underscore a critical point: Christian Zionism is not a denomination. It is not a religion. It is an ideology, one that fuses theology with geopolitics, prophecy with policy, and belief with power.

This book is not an attack on faith. It is a plea to rescue it from distortion. It is an invitation to separate the sacred from the strategic, the spiritual from the supremacist, and the prophetic from the political. It is a call to restore empathy, justice, and truth to the heart of our religious and moral imagination.

If you are a person of faith, I ask you to read with an open heart. If you are a skeptic, I ask you to read with an open mind. And if you are someone who has ever felt the "switch in the mind", that moment when empathy shuts down in the name of belief, I ask you to consider flipping it back on.

Let us begin.

**Bilal Shammout**

# Introduction: A Switch in the Mind

I did not set out to write a book. I set out to understand something I could not explain.

In the late 1980s, I arrived in the United States to begin my university studies. I eventually settled in Charlotte, North Carolina, often called the buckle of the Bible Belt. At the time, I didn't know what that meant. But over the years, I came to realize how deeply it shaped the conversations I had, the friendships I formed, and the questions that led to this book.

One aspect of my life in the U.S. felt like a scene from the movie *Groundhog Day*. Almost every day, someone, usually a white American, would notice my accent and ask where I was from. I'd say, "I'm Palestinian," and almost always, they'd respond, "Pakestinian?" I'd clarify, "No, Palestinian. From Palestine." Their puzzled expression would follow: "Palestine? Where is that? I've never heard of it." I'd ask, "Do you know Jerusalem?" and they'd immediately light up: "Yes! Ah, you're Israeli." Sometimes they'd say Jewish. I'd reply, "No, Israel is occupying Palestine."

Most of the time, that ended the conversation. But occasionally, if they were curious and time allowed, they'd ask, "What do you mean Israel is occupying Palestine?" I'd spend the next 45 minutes giving a history lesson, often sharing how my parents were exiled from their homes and became refugees at a young age. And yet, no matter how compelling or heartfelt the conversation was, it almost always ended the same way. Something would shift. It's hard to describe, like a switch flipping in their minds, telling them: you should not empathize any further.

On rare occasions, the conversation continued. One of those rare exceptions was Clark.

We met while working at a large multinational company. Clark was a gentle soul and a devout Christian. Our first conversation followed the usual pattern, the switch flipped, and the topic faded. But over time, we became close friends and colleagues. He often asked me about Islam, and I shared what I knew. In one of our early exchanges, I asked if he was Catholic. Offended, he replied sharply, "No man, I'm Christian." I apologized, still unsure of the difference.

As our friendship grew, I often spoke to Clark about the Israeli occupation and the peace process. In September 2000, the Second Intifada erupted in the occupied Palestinian territories. For seven years since the Oslo Accords, Israel, backed by Western powers, especially the U.S., had delayed serious negotiations. The trigger came when Israeli Prime Minister Ariel Sharon entered Masjid Al-Aqsa in Jerusalem, Islam's third holiest site. This move was unprecedented, provocative, and symbolic. It signaled that Israel had no intention of honoring the Oslo agreement's promise of a future Palestinian state with East Jerusalem as its capital.

The next day, the uprising began. Israeli forces responded with brutal force. By December, the situation was worsening daily. I followed the news closely and kept Clark updated. One day, I took a break from work and opened CNN's website. The headline stunned me: leaders of major Christian denominations in the U.S. had signed a letter, prepared by an organization called Christians United for Israel (CUFI), expressing support for Israel.

I felt sick. I went downstairs for a cigarette. Clark happened to pass by and noticed my expression.

"What's wrong?" he asked. "You look upset."

"I am," I said. "I've lived in this country for 13 years, and I still don't understand it. Americans talk endlessly about democracy, human rights, freedom of speech, and the rule of law. But after everything happening in Palestine, the brutality, the injustice, Christian leaders here issue a letter defending Israel. I just don't understand this country anymore."

Clark looked at me with empathy and said, "Some people are stupid. They think they can speed up God."

Confused, I asked, "What do you mean?"

He replied, "You know, we have a prophecy that says Jesus is supposed to come back. And some people think they can make that happen faster."

Even more confused, I said, "You know what, man? I don't understand this stuff, and I guess I never will."

That was the end of the conversation. But months later, after I had moved away from the U.S. and resettled into a new life, I remembered Clark's words. They echoed in my mind. Speed up God. What did that mean? Why did Christians, especially in America, support Israel so fervently? Why not Christians elsewhere?

That question became the spark.

I began researching, reading, and asking questions. What started as curiosity became a 12-year journey, one that led me to uncover the roots, history, and global impact of a movement few truly understand: Christian Zionism.

This book is the result of that journey. It is not a theological critique. I am not a theologian. I do not claim to speak for any faith tradition. I am simply trying to share what I have lived, what I have learned, and what I now understand.

This book is not about doctrine. It is about empathy. It is about the switch in the mind, and how we might turn it back on.

## Why This Book Matters Now

We are living in a time of deepening division, religious, political, and moral. The term Christian Zionism is increasingly heard in media, pulpits, and policy debates. Yet few understand what it truly means, where it came from, or how profoundly it shapes our world.

This book was born out of personal experience, not theological expertise. I am not a scholar of religion. I am a Palestinian who spent years trying to understand why empathy for my people so often vanished in conversations with well-meaning Christians. Why did support for Israel override concern for justice? Why did suffering become invisible when prophecy was invoked?

What I discovered was not just a belief system, but a worldview. One that quietly influences foreign policy, distorts scripture, and numbs moral conscience. One that turns theology into strategy and faith into justification for violence.

Christian Zionism is not just a theological position. It is a political engine. It has shaped culture, media, and diplomacy, especially in the United States, and continues to drive events in the Middle East and beyond. Scholars like Stephen Sizer have warned that it is a roadmap to geopolitical disaster. This book picks up where those critiques left off, not to debate doctrine, but to expose how this ideology has impacted real lives, especially Palestinian lives.

Understanding Christian Zionism is no longer optional. It is essential for anyone who wants to grasp the deeper forces behind global alliances, religious movements, and the persistent conflict over Palestine.

This book is not an attack on faith. It is a call to reclaim it. It is an invitation to restore empathy, justice, and truth to the heart of our moral imagination.

## What to expect

**A Quick HeadsUp:** Because this book engages with specialized language from theology, history, and politics, you'll find a detailed glossary at the end. If you come across a term that seems unfamiliar, don't worry, the glossary is your guide. Feel free to flip to it anytime as you read.

This book is not a theological treatise. It is a personal journey, one shaped by lived experience, years of research, and a deep desire to understand a belief system that has profoundly impacted my life and the lives of millions of others.

You will not find doctrinal arguments or theological debates here. What you will find is a careful, respectful, and morally urgent exploration of how Christian Zionism, a theological-political ideology, came to be, how it evolved, and how it continues to shape global events, especially in relation to Palestine.

This book will take you through history, theology, politics, and culture. Along the way, you will learn:

- How Christian Zionism predates Jewish Zionism by over sixty years.
- Why Protestant movements in Europe laid the foundation for apocalyptic thinking and biblical literalism.
- How dispensationalism reshaped Christian theology and gave rise to a political agenda.
- The hidden role of Christian figures in supporting the establishment of a Jewish homeland in Palestine.

- How American religious culture, through media, politics, and education, became fertile ground for Christian Zionist ideology.
- Why the push to rebuild Solomon's Temple is not just a Jewish fundamentalist dream, but a Christian Zionist imperative.
- And most importantly, how this belief system poses a grave and often misunderstood threat to global peace, interfaith understanding, and moral conscience.

This book is not an attack on faith. It is a call to reclaim it. It is an invitation to examine how belief can be used to justify harm, and how we might restore empathy, justice, and truth to the center of our spiritual and political lives.

To understand how Christian Zionism came to be, and why it holds such sway over American politics, media, and religious thought, we must begin not in the modern era, but in the heart of Europe during the Protestant Reformation. It was there, in the struggle to translate the Bible from Latin into local languages, that the seeds of Christian Zionism were first sown.

But before we begin, here is a word from the Church.

# A Word from the Church:
# Archbishop Atallah Hanna Speaks

Before we begin exploring the roots and reach of Christian Zionism, it is important to hear from one of the most courageous voices of the Church in our time. Archbishop Atallah Hanna, Greek Orthodox Archbishop of Sebastia - Palestine, has spoken with clarity and conviction about the dangers of Christian Zionism, not only for Palestine, but for Christianity itself.

His words matter because they come from the heart of the Holy Land, from a leader who embodies the oldest Christian presence in the world. They resonate deeply with the thesis of this book: that Christian Zionism is not a harmless theological curiosity, but a formidable force that distorts faith, sanctifies injustice, and erases empathy. To confront it, we must first understand what it is, and why voices like Archbishop Hanna's reject it so unequivocally.

Here is his statement in full:

# We do not recognize what is called "Christian Zionism." You are either a Christian or a Zionist.

**M**any ask us: *What is the position of your churches regarding the groups that call themselves "Christian Zionists"?* The answer is: We do not recognize this term. In our Christian ecclesiastical vocabulary, there is no such designation as "Christian Zionists." You are either a Christian or a Zionist. The attempt to merge Christianity and Zionism is completely rejected and condemned.

Christianity is a religion of mercy, love, humanity, and peace. Zionism, on the other hand, is a racist movement that has caused the catastrophes and tragedies suffered by our Palestinian people. Those who call themselves "Christian Zionists", we are not obliged to adopt this term, which we absolutely reject. Their literature, for anyone who reads it, is alien to the pinnacle of Christian values and principles. They exist to harm Christianity and to manipulate Old Testament texts for Zionist interests, thereby distorting its teachings, which we do not view it as part of the New Testament.

When these people come to the Holy Land, they do not meet with our churches, nor with Palestinian Christians, nor do they visit the Church of the Holy Sepulchre in Jerusalem or the Church of the Nativity in Bethlehem, because they do not recognize these holy sites. Instead, they go to settlements and colonies in the Golan and the West Bank to show solidarity with the occupying settlers who violate the freedom and dignity of the Palestinian people.

The most outrageous insult to Christianity is to call these people "Christian Zionists." I prefer the term: *Zionist individuals falsely claiming to belong to Christianity.* The recent genocide that destroyed Gaza and caused immense pain, sorrow, tears, and blood has exposed many masks and unveiled many faces.

To be a Christian means to stand for truth and justice, to defend the oppressed, and to embody noble human values. Yesterday's Gospel reading in our holy churches was the parable of the Good Samaritan, who showed compassion to a wounded man he encountered on the road between Jerusalem and Jericho. What that Samaritan saw can be seen by anyone in this world, wherever there is pain, sorrow, hardship, and suffering, our alignment must be with those whom our Holy Scripture calls "the little brothers of Jesus." Those who turn a blind eye to the suffering of our people, or any oppressed people, cannot be true Christians, because authentic Christianity calls us to be a voice for truth, justice, and defense of the oppressed.

I say to Christians worldwide, as you prepare to celebrate the glorious Christmas season: turn your attention to Palestine, its wounds, and the suffering of its people. This is a profoundly Christian cause and cannot be reduced to a mere political issue. To defend Palestine in its ordeal, pain, and wounds means defending the oldest Christian presence in the world, the Mother of Churches, and the first church built in this blessed land, from which the message of faith spread everywhere.

Those who falsely call themselves "Christian Zionists" are, before being enemies of anything else, enemies of Christianity and its values and principles. We do not wish them harm; rather, we pray for their guidance, repentance, and return to the true Christianity that calls for love, mercy, humanity, and peace.

The genocide and the suffering of our people have exposed these factions aligned with the occupation, and their influence is declining day by day because we believe that the power of truth is stronger than the power of falsehood. I was very glad to hear yesterday from an American Jewish thinker who supports justice, saying that the targeting of Palestinians and what happened in Gaza is a war against Judaism, Christianity, and Islam, because this injustice and these oppressive, racist practices contradict the values upheld by the three monotheistic religions.

How beautiful it is when believers of all faiths unite in defending Palestine, truth, justice, and peace, and in calling for an end to the injustices suffered by Palestinians in every aspect of their lives. We always welcome delegations in solidarity with our people, some even go to the West Bank to support olive harvesters. These people come from all religions, races, and cultural backgrounds, united by the suffering of our Palestinian people.

I repeat and clarify: we do not recognize what is called "Christian Zionism." You are either a Christian or a Zionist. Mixing good and evil is an equation that cannot be accepted, justified, or surrendered to in any way. We pray that God guides these people to the path of faith, truth, mercy, humanity, and peace. Instead of siding with the oppressor, they should side with the oppressed and call for lifting the injustice from them.

We do not believe in the concept of a "chosen people." All peoples are chosen, they are God's creation. There is no first-class human and tenth-class human; all humans are brothers in their shared humanity, and everyone has the right to live in security and peace, far from the machinery of death, destruction, and wars. Our Palestinian people deserve to live in freedom and peace, and these injustices, which peaked with the genocide and the suffering they endure in every detail of their lives, must not continue.

How much we need God's mercy in these difficult times, where the freedom and dignity of the Palestinian person are violated, and they are made to feel like strangers in their own homeland. The Palestinian is not a stranger in his homeland, nor an outsider or imported commodity. Palestinians deserve to live in their homeland and to be free, far from the machinery of death, racism, and targeting that undermine their normal lives in every detail.

**Archbishop Atallah Hanna**

Greek Orthodox Archbishop of Sebastia

November 24, 2025

*Translated from Arabic and reprinted in full with permission from Archbishop Atallah Hanna, Facebook post dated November 24, 2025.*

The Archbishop's words are a moral compass, a call to clarity in a time of confusion. They remind us that Christian Zionism is not a theological nuance but a distortion with profound consequences for faith, justice, and humanity. Yet to confront this ideology effectively, we must do more than condemn it. We must understand it, its origins, its evolution, and the forces that have carried it from obscure prophecy circles to the halls of power. That journey begins now, as we trace the seeds of interpretation that gave rise to one of the most influential, and dangerous, theological movements of the modern era.

# Part I

# The Seeds of Interpretation

# Chapter 1

## From Empire to Ecclesia
## The Birth of the Roman Church
## and the Foundations of Christian Zionism

Before we begin, it's important to clarify three key terms: **Zionism, Jewish Zionism, and Christian Zionism. While all three share a common destination, the establishment of a Jewish homeland, their motivations, origins, and implications differ significantly.** This book focuses on **Christian Zionism**, a theological-political ideology that has shaped global events in ways often misunderstood.

To understand the theological and political roots of Christian Zionism, we must begin **not in the 20th century, nor even during the Protestant Reformation, but in the early centuries of Christianity, when a persecuted spiritual movement became the official religion of the Roman Empire.** This transformation, orchestrated by emperors and theologians, laid the groundwork for the institutional Church, the canonization of scripture, and the theological frameworks that would later be used, sometimes weaponized, in service of empire and prophecy.

This chapter is not a critique of Christianity. It is an exploration of how theology and power became intertwined, and how that entanglement created conditions that would eventually give rise to Christian Zionism.

## Christianity Before Rome

Long before the rise of the Roman Catholic Church, Christianity had already taken root across the Eastern Mediterranean. The **Eastern Orthodox Churches, including Greek, Syriac, Coptic, and Armenian traditions, trace their origins to the earliest followers of Jesus.** These communities preserved Christ's teachings in their native languages, worshipped in local liturgical traditions, and developed theological schools that shaped early Christian doctrine.

The Orthodox tradition emphasizes the continuity of apostolic teaching, the mystical experience of God, and the communal nature of salvation. Unlike the Roman Church, which centralized authority in the papacy, the Orthodox Churches maintained a conciliar model of leadership, with patriarchs and bishops sharing ecclesiastical authority. This distinction is crucial: while both traditions claim apostolic succession, the Orthodox Churches predate the Roman Catholic Church as an institution and offer a different lens through which to understand scripture, tradition, and authority.

## Constantine and the Legalization of Christianity

A pivotal moment in Christianity's transformation came in **313 CE**, when Emperor Constantine the Great issued the **Edict of Milan**, granting religious tolerance to Christians throughout the Roman Empire (MacCulloch, 2010). This act ended centuries of persecution and marked the beginning of Christianity's ascent to political power.

But Constantine's role went far beyond tolerance. In 325 CE, he convened the First Council of Nicaea to unify Christian doctrine and suppress theological disputes that threatened imperial stability. The council produced the Nicene

Creed, a foundational statement of Christian belief, and established the precedent for imperial involvement in theological matters.

Constantine saw Christianity not merely as a spiritual force but as a strategic tool to unify the empire. His vision culminated in the formation of what would become the Roman Catholic Church, a centralized, hierarchical institution with the Bishop of Rome (later the Pope) at its head (Brown, 1989).

## Canonizing the Bible: A Library, Not a Book

One of Constantine's most enduring legacies was the canonization of Christian scripture. Contrary to popular belief, the Bible is not a single book, but a library of texts written over centuries by diverse authors in Hebrew, Aramaic, and Greek (McDonald & Sanders, 2002). These include historical chronicles, poetry, prophecy, law codes, letters, and apocalyptic visions.

Determining which books belonged in the Bible was a complex and contested process. Different Christian communities recognized different texts as authoritative. The Council of Nicaea and subsequent synods helped shape the canon, but the final list varied between traditions. To this day, Catholic, Orthodox, and Protestant Bibles differ in content and structure (Metzger, 1987).

This diversity is not a flaw, it is a testament to the richness of the Christian tradition. But it also means that interpretation has always been central to Christian faith. The Bible is not a monolith; it is a mosaic of voices, genres, and historical contexts.

## The Book of Revelation: Apocalypse and Interpretation

Among the most enigmatic and influential texts in the biblical canon is the Book of Revelation, also known as the Apocalypse of John. Written in the late first century CE, Revelation presents a symbolic vision of cosmic conflict, divine judgment, and ultimate redemption (Revelation 20–22).

For centuries, Revelation was read allegorically or spiritually, especially within Orthodox and Catholic traditions. It was seen as a poetic meditation on the struggle between good and evil, not a literal roadmap to the end of the world.

However, during the Protestant Reformation and the rise of dispensationalist theology, Revelation began to be read literally, as a prophetic script detailing future events, including the Rapture, the Tribulation, the rise of the Antichrist, and the battle of Armageddon (Kyle, 2012; Blaising & Bock, 1993). This shift had profound consequences. It transformed Revelation from a mystical vision into a geopolitical strategy, one later used to justify war, colonization, and the dispossession of entire peoples.

Orthodox and Catholic Churches continue to interpret Revelation symbolically, emphasizing its spiritual and liturgical dimensions. They caution against speculative prophecy and reject the idea that human actions can hasten the end times. This stands in stark contrast to Christian Zionist theology, which treats Revelation as a divine playbook to be enacted on the world stage.

## St. Jerome and the Latin Vulgate

To consolidate the Church's authority, Constantine commissioned the translation of the newly canonized scriptures into Latin, the official language of the empire. This task fell to St. Jerome, who completed the Vulgate translation in the late fourth century (Jerome, 390/2005).

The Vulgate became the official Bible of the Catholic Church and remained so for over a millennium. Latin, inaccessible to the common people, became the exclusive medium of scripture, liturgy, and theology. This linguistic barrier ensured that only the educated elite, primarily the clergy, could read and interpret the Bible.

This monopoly on scripture was not merely linguistic, it was a mechanism of control. By restricting access to the Bible, the Church positioned itself as the sole mediator between God and humanity. This control would later be challenged by reformers who sought to return scripture to the people.

## The Rise of Ecclesiastical Power and the Seeds of Corruption

With the collapse of the Western Roman Empire in 476 CE, most political institutions disintegrated. But the Catholic Church endured. It preserved Roman administrative structures, rituals, and language. The Pope emerged as both a spiritual and temporal authority, often wielding more power than kings and emperors (MacCulloch, 2010).

This concentration of power led to centuries of corruption. The Church became entangled in politics, wealth, and warfare. One of the most egregious abuses was the sale of indulgences, certificates that promised the remission of sins in exchange for money. These indulgences were marketed as spiritual guarantees, turning salvation into a commodity.

The sale of indulgences was not an isolated scandal, it was a symptom of deeper rot. The Church's monopoly on scripture, its alliance with imperial power, and its unchecked authority created a system ripe for exploitation. The spiritual became political. The sacred became transactional.

The sale of indulgences began in the 11th century and peaked during the 14th to 16th centuries, becoming a major source of Church revenue. These certificates, sold with papal approval, promised reduced punishment for sins and were marketed as spiritual guarantees. The funds raised were used to finance Church operations, including lavish clerical lifestyles and monumental projects like the construction of St. Peter's Basilica in Rome. Though initially framed as acts of charity, indulgences evolved into a transactional system that commodified salvation. The practice was officially abolished in 1567 by Pope Pius V, but not before it had sparked widespread outrage and helped ignite the Protestant Reformation.

## A Turning Point Ahead

This is the world into which the Protestant Reformation erupted, a world where access to scripture was restricted, where theology served empire, and where the Church's power was absolute. The grievances that fueled the Reformation were not merely doctrinal, they were moral, political, and deeply human.

In the next chapter, we will explore how reformers like Martin Luther and William Tyndale challenged the Church's monopoly on truth, demanded access to scripture, and laid the foundations for a new kind of Christianity, one that would eventually give rise to Christian Zionism.

# Chapter 2
## The Reformation
## When the Bible Broke Free

The Catholic Church's dominance over medieval Europe was not merely spiritual, it was **total and pervasive**. With the collapse of the Western Roman Empire, the Church emerged as the sole surviving institution, wielding both religious and political power. The Pope crowned kings, dictated moral law, and controlled the keys to salvation. But with absolute power came absolute corruption.

## The Church in Crisis: Power, Profit, and the Price of Salvation

By the late Middle Ages, the Catholic Church had become a vast empire unto itself. Its wealth rivaled that of monarchs, its cathedrals towered over cities, and its priests and bishops lived in luxury while the masses toiled in poverty. One of the most egregious abuses was the sale of indulgences, certificates that promised forgiveness of sins in exchange for money.

The Church's monopoly on the interpretation of scripture made such abuses possible. The Bible was written and read exclusively in Latin, a language inaccessible to the common people. Only the clergy could read it, and only the Church could explain it. This meant that the faithful were entirely dependent on priests to understand God's word, and the priests, in turn, were often more interested in preserving power than preaching truth.

## Martin Luther: The Monk Who Lit the Fuse

Into this world of spiritual decay stepped **Martin Luther**, a German monk, theologian, and professor. Born in 1483 in Eisleben, Germany, Luther was the son of a miner who hoped his son would become a lawyer. But after a near-death experience during a thunderstorm, Luther vowed to become a monk. He joined the Augustinian order, eventually earning a doctorate in theology and teaching at the University of Wittenberg.

Luther was a devout man, tormented by a deep sense of unworthiness before God. He immersed himself in scripture, seeking solace and truth. What he found instead was a Church that had strayed far from the teachings of Christ. The final straw came in 1517, when a Dominican friar named Johann Tetzel began selling indulgences in Germany with the slogan: *"As soon as the coin in the coffer rings, the soul from purgatory springs."*

Outraged, Luther penned a document that would change the course of history.

*Martin Luther, (1483-1528)*

## The 95 Theses: A Call for Reform

On **October 31, 1517**, Luther nailed his **95 Theses** to the door of the Castle Church in Wittenberg. These were not radical demands for revolution, they were an invitation to debate. Written in Latin, the Theses challenged the theological basis for indulgences and questioned the Church's authority to forgive sins for money.

To a modern reader, the 95 Theses might seem like a list of academic complaints. But in Luther's time, they were explosive. He argued that salvation came not through the Church's rituals or payments, but through faith alone (*sola fide*). He insisted that the Bible, not the Pope, was the ultimate authority in matters of faith (*sola scriptura*). And most importantly, he believed that every Christian had the right to read and interpret scripture for themselves.

## The Bible in the People's Tongue

Luther understood that as long as the Bible remained in Latin, the Church would retain its stranglehold on truth. So he set out to translate the Bible into German, the language of the people. Working from the original Hebrew and Greek texts, Luther completed the New Testament in 1522 and the full Bible by 1534 (MacCulloch, 2010). His translation was not only a theological act, it was a cultural revolution. It helped standardize the German language and empowered ordinary people to engage with scripture directly.

Inspired by Luther's example, others followed suit. In England, a scholar named William Tyndale took up the same mission.

## William Tyndale: The Martyr of the English Bible

Born around 1494, **William Tyndale** was a brilliant linguist and priest who believed that every Englishman should be able to read the Bible in his own language. He famously declared to a clergyman, *"If God spare my life, ere many years I will cause a boy that driveth the plough to know more of the Scripture than thou dost."*

Tyndale translated the New Testament into Old English directly from the Greek, bypassing the Latin Vulgate. His translation was smuggled into England in bales of cloth and read in secret by eager believers. But the Catholic Church saw this as heresy. In 1536, Tyndale was betrayed, arrested, and burned at the stake. His final words were, *"Lord, open the King of England's eyes."*

Ironically, just a few years later, King Henry VIII authorized the Great Bible, which was based largely on Tyndale's work. His sacrifice had not been in vain.

*William Tyndale, (1494-1536)*

## The Printing Press: A Divine Disruption

The Reformation might have remained a fringe movement were it not for a technological marvel: **the printing press**. Invented by Johannes Gutenberg in the mid-15th century, the press revolutionized the spread of information. Before its invention, Bibles were copied by hand, an expensive and time-consuming process. A single Bible could take years to produce and cost more than a house.

With the printing press, Luther's German Bible and Tyndale's English New Testament could be mass-produced and distributed widely. For the first time, ordinary people could own a Bible, read it in their own language, and form their own understanding of God's word (Eisenstein, 1980).

This democratization of scripture was both liberating and destabilizing.

## The Rise of Interpretive Christianity

Once the Bible was in the hands of the people, a new era began, **one of interpretive Christianity**. No longer bound by the Church's official teachings, believers began to read scripture for themselves. And with personal reading came personal interpretation.

The result was a theological explosion. The Protestant movement, which began as an attempt to reform the Catholic Church, soon splintered into dozens, and eventually hundreds, of denominations. Some emphasized grace, others focused on prophecy. Some embraced symbolic readings of scripture, while others insisted on literalism.

This fragmentation was both a strength and a weakness. On one hand, it allowed for a diversity of thought and a rejection of centralized authority. On the other, it created confusion, division, and competing claims to truth. The Bible, once chained in Latin behind church walls, was now a battlefield of ideas.

The Reformation did more than liberate the Bible from Latin, it unleashed a theological revolution that rippled across centuries. As sacred texts became accessible to the masses, a new kind of Christianity emerged, one rooted not in ecclesiastical authority, but in personal interpretation. This democratization of scripture, while empowering, also opened the floodgates to a torrent of eschatological speculation.

In the next chapter, we explore how this shift gave rise to a profound obsession with the end of days, an obsession that would shape Protestant theology, fuel apocalyptic movements, and lay the groundwork for Christian Zionism.

# Chapter 3
## The Obsession with the End
## Protestant Eschatology
## and the Second Coming

A mong the most potent and enduring ideas to emerge was the belief in the Second Coming, the conviction that Jesus Christ would return to Earth to judge the living and the dead, ushering in a new divine order.

## From Reformation to Revelation: A Shift in Focus

In Catholic and Orthodox traditions, the Second Coming was acknowledged but not emphasized. It was a distant, mysterious event, part of the creeds, yes, but not a central focus of daily faith. The Catholic Church, with its emphasis on sacramental life and ecclesiastical mediation, discouraged lay speculation on eschatology. The Orthodox Churches, rooted in mysticism and liturgical continuity, interpreted apocalyptic texts like Revelation symbolically, emphasizing spiritual vigilance over prophetic calculation.

But for Protestants, especially those influenced by the radical wings of the Reformation, the Second Coming became a theological lodestar. With the collapse of centralized interpretive authority, believers turned to the Bible not just for moral guidance, but for clues. They scoured the prophetic books, Daniel, Ezekiel, Revelation, seeking signs, timelines, and divine blueprints. The question was no longer *if* Christ would return, but *when, how*, and *what must be done to prepare*.

This obsession was not confined to the fringes. Contrary to popular belief, it was not merely the domain of fanatics or simpletons. Some of the most brilliant minds of the Enlightenment era were captivated by the mysteries of prophecy.

## Isaac Newton: The Scientist and the Seer

Among the most surprising of these was **Sir Isaac Newton, the father of modern physics, discoverer of gravity, and inventor of calculus**. While Newton is celebrated for his scientific genius, few know that he devoted more time to theology than to science. He spent two decades developing calculus to describe the laws of motion, but he spent over four decades calculating the date of the Second Coming.

Newton poured his intellect into deciphering the Bible, convinced that its prophetic texts contained a hidden code revealing the precise timeline of divine history. In his posthumously published work, *Observations upon the Prophecies of Daniel and the Apocalypse of St. John* (1733), Newton argued that the Bible was a cryptic historical record written in advance by God. He believed that by applying mathematical rigor to scripture, just as he had done with physics, he could unlock the divine timeline of history (Newton, 1991). His calculations led him to predict that the end of the world would not occur before the year 2060 (Keynes, 1946).

Newton's theological pursuits were not an eccentric hobby, they were central to his worldview. He saw no contradiction between science and scripture. For him, both were revelations of divine order: one through nature, the other through prophecy. His work exemplifies the intellectual seriousness with which many

Protestants approached eschatology. The Second Coming was not a metaphor, it was a solvable equation.

## The Jewish Question and the Christian Answer

As Protestant eschatology matured over the following two centuries, it gave rise to a proliferation of prophetic societies, Bible study groups, and missionary organizations, all dedicated to answering three burning questions: *When will Christ return? How will it happen? What must be done to prepare?*

During this period, many of these groups began to focus on the role of the Jewish people in the Second Coming. Eventually, they splintered into two main camps. One believed that the Second Coming would not occur unless the Jews accepted Jesus as the Messiah. The other believed that the Jews must be physically restored to Palestine, regardless of their religious beliefs.

Both views were rooted in a literal reading of prophecy and a conviction that human action could hasten divine fulfillment.

## Societies of the End: Organizing for the Apocalypse

One of the most influential groups advocating for Jewish conversion was the **London Society for Promoting Christianity Amongst the Jews**, commonly called **London Jews Society (LJS)**, founded in 1809. While its stated mission was evangelistic, to convert Jews to Christianity, its underlying motivation was eschatological. Many of its founders believed that the conversion of the Jews was a necessary precondition for the Second Coming (Ariel, 2013).

The LJS was not an isolated phenomenon. It was part of a broader movement that saw the Jewish people as central to God's end-times plan.

By the early 19th century, **evangelicalism** was thriving within Protestantism. Evangelicals emphasized personal conversion, the authority of scripture, and the urgency of spreading the gospel. Their theology was often marked by biblical literalism and a deep concern with eschatology, the study of the end times.

Evangelicalism was not a denomination, but a movement that spanned across Baptist, Methodist, Anglican, and other Protestant traditions. It created fertile ground for apocalyptic thinking and prophetic speculation, setting the stage for Darby's dispensationalist framework.

## John Nelson Darby and the Restorationist Turn

Among the most influential Restorationists was **John Nelson Darby**, an Anglican priest turned dissenter who would go on to develop the theological system known as **dispensationalism**.

In the next chapter, we will explore how Darby's dispensationalism became the scaffolding of Christian Zionist belief, and how it redefined the relationship between prophecy, politics, and power.

# Chapter 4
## John Nelson Darby and
## the Framework of Dispensationalism

A s Protestant Europe became increasingly obsessed with prophecy and the Second Coming, a new theological framework emerged to organize and interpret biblical history: **dispensationalism**. Developed by **John Nelson Darby** in the 19th century, this system offered a structured timeline of divine activity and provided a blueprint for understanding the past, present, and future through a prophetic lens. **Dispensationalism would become the theological backbone of Christian Zionism, shaping evangelical thought in Europe and North America for generations.**

## John Nelson Darby: Background and Beliefs

**John Nelson Darby (1800–1882)** was shaped by both scholarship and solitude. Educated at Westminster School and Trinity College Dublin, he was ordained as an Anglican priest in the Church of Ireland. After a fall from a horse in 1827 left him bedridden, Darby entered a period of deep reflection. He began to question the institutional church and immersed himself in scripture. From this emerged a radically new theological framework that would reshape Protestant eschatology and lay the foundation for Christian Zionism.

*John N. Darby, (1800-1882)*

Darby's theology rested on two core assumptions:

- **The Bible is the literal word of God**, he insisted the bible should be read and understood literally not metaphorically, symbolically, spiritually, or allegorically as has been done for centuries. He treated the King James Version (KJV) as divinely authoritative.

- **The Bible is a book of human history written in advance by God**, containing everything that has happened, is happening, and will happen.

Perhaps Darby's most radical departure from traditional Christian theology was his rejection of the long standing Replacement theology in Christendom.

Replacement theology, also known as *supersessionism*, teaches that the Christian Church has replaced Israel as God's chosen people. According to this view, since the Jews rejected Jesus as the Messiah, the covenants, promises, and blessings originally given to Israel in the Hebrew Bible are now fulfilled in the Church (Soulen, 1996). This theology became dominant in both Catholic and Protestant traditions and contributed to antisemitic attitudes by framing Jewish identity as obsolete or spiritually inferior (Ariel, 2013).

Darby insisted on a **permanent separation between Israel and the Church**. He argued that the promises made to Israel in the Old Testament were not transferred to the Church but remained valid and would be fulfilled in the future (Sandeen, 1970).

Darby's framework reintroduced Israel as a central figure in eschatology, laying the groundwork for Christian Zionist support for Jewish restoration to Palestine. This theological distinction would later justify unwavering political support for the modern state of Israel, regardless of its policies or actions.

## Biblical Israel vs. the Modern State of Israel

One of the most persistent assumptions in Christian Zionist theology is the conflation of **Biblical Israel** with the **modern state of Israel**. While they share a name and geographic overlap, they are fundamentally different.

- **Biblical Israel** refers to the ancient covenant community described in the Hebrew Bible, descendants of Abraham, Isaac, and Jacob, chosen by God to live according to divine law and serve as a light to the nations (Genesis 12:1–3; Exodus 19:5–6). It was a theological construct, not a modern nation-state (Soulen, 1996).

- **Modern Israel**, established in 1948, is a political entity shaped by diplomacy, military conflict, and nationalist ideology. It is governed by secular law and composed of diverse ethnic and religious groups (Laqueur, 2003).

Dispensationalists often treat modern Israel as the direct fulfillment of biblical prophecy, citing verses like Genesis 12:3, "I will bless those who bless you…", as divine endorsements of Israeli statehood. But this interpretation collapses centuries of theological development and ignores the historical and political realities of Zionism (Spector, 2009).

This conflation turns political support into spiritual obligation, sanctifies military actions as divine mandates, and erases the distinction between ancient covenant theology and modern nationalism.

## The Seven Dispensations

With these assumptions, and this mindset, Darby began reading the Bible not as a spiritual guide, but as a chronological blueprint. He started seeing a pattern in the bible that no one else saw before.

He identified a cyclical pattern of divine interaction with humanity: God issues a command, humanity fails, God responds with judgment, and a new cycle begins. He called these cycles **dispensations**, seven distinct phases in God's relationship with humanity:

### 1. Dispensation of Innocence
### Genesis 1–3

God created Adam and Eve and placed them in the Garden of Eden in direct communion with Him. They lived in complete moral innocence. God gave them one command: do not eat from the Tree of the Knowledge of Good and Evil. They disobeyed. The Fall occurred. God expelled them from Eden. This marked the first divine judgment and the end of the first dispensation.

## 2. Dispensation of Conscience
### Genesis 4–8
From the Fall to the Flood, humanity was expected to live righteously, guided by conscience. But sin multiplied rapidly. Cain murdered Abel. Corruption spread. Genesis 6 describes a world so wicked that God judged it with a catastrophic flood, sparing only Noah and his family.

## 3. Dispensation of Human Government
### Genesis 9–11
After the flood, God gave Noah and his descendants the authority to govern and enforce justice, including capital punishment. But humanity again failed. At the Tower of Babel, people sought to elevate themselves and unify under human ambition. God responded by confusing their languages and scattering them across the earth.

## 4. Dispensation of Promise
### Genesis 12–Exodus 19
God chose Abraham and made a covenant with him: land, descendants, and blessing. This dispensation emphasized faith and obedience. But the Israelites fell into idolatry and disobedience during their time in Egypt. Their failure led to enslavement and the need for divine deliverance.

## 5. Dispensation of Law
### Exodus 20–John 19
God gave the Israelites the Mosaic Law, a comprehensive set of religious, moral, and civil commandments. This era was marked by strict legalism and sacrificial rituals. Despite prophetic warnings, Israel repeatedly broke the covenant. The ultimate failure was the rejection of Jesus as the Messiah, which dispensationalists view as the end of the Law era and the beginning of the Church Age.

## 6. Dispensation of Grace (Church Age)
### Acts 2–Present
This is the current era. God's expectation is that humanity will accept Jesus as Lord and Savior and live by the grace of the Church. But Darby observed that most of humanity has not, and will not, meet this expectation. Therefore, as in every previous dispensation, divine judgment must follow. This judgment will come in the form of a global catastrophe that ushers in the final dispensation.

## 7. Dispensation of the Kingdom (Millennial Reign)
### Revelation 20
This final dispensation begins after Jesus returns to Earth, defeats the Antichrist in the battle of Armageddon, and "removes" (i.e., kills) all non-believers. Jesus then establishes His kingdom on Earth, ruling from Jerusalem for a literal

1,000 years. Only believers remain. Humanity lives in peace and harmony. After the millennium, the final judgment occurs, and all of humanity is saved, having accepted Christ and lived according to God's expectations.

## The Prophetic Roadmap: Nine Steps to the End

Once Darby saw this pattern, he began thinking backwards from the seventh dispensation. What had to happen for it to begin? He concluded that the final dispensation would only start after Jesus defeats the Antichrist in the battle of Armageddon. But that battle is the climax of a seven-year global war called the **Tribulation**, marked by unprecedented suffering, wars, famine, disease, and chaos.

This posed a theological problem: if the Tribulation is global, what happens to believers? Would they suffer too? To address this conundrum, Darby invented a new concept that never existed in Christendom, the **Rapture**. At the start of the Tribulation, Jesus would lift His believers to heaven, sparing them from the horrors on Earth. Then, at the end of the Tribulation, Jesus would return with His army of believers and defeat the Antichrist.

But what triggers the Tribulation? According to Darby, it begins when a charismatic global leader, the Antichrist, brokers peace in the Middle East and helps rebuild the Jewish temple in Jerusalem. This peace is false. The Antichrist desecrates the temple by declaring himself divine, triggering the global war.

This led Darby to a sequence of **nine prophetic steps** that must occur before the final dispensation begins:

- **Restoration of the Jews**: A homeland must be created for the Jewish people in the Promised Land.

- **Conflict with Neighbours**: This homeland must be in constant conflict, requiring military superiority.*

- **Security and Immigration**: Israel must be secure enough to attract global Jewish immigration.*

- **Peace Deal and Temple Rebuilding**: The Antichrist brokers peace and helps rebuild the temple.

- **Desecration of the Temple**: The Antichrist declares himself divine, triggering the Tribulation.

- **Rapture of Believers**: Jesus lifts His followers to heaven before or at the start of the Tribulation.

- **144,000 Jewish Evangelists**: During the Tribulation, 144,000 Jews accept Jesus and evangelize. **

- **Second Coming of Christ**: Jesus returns with His army and defeats the Antichrist at Armageddon.

- **Final Judgment and Kingdom**: Non-believers are removed. Jesus establishes His kingdom in Jerusalem for 1,000 years. Afterward, all humanity is saved.

  \* These points are not explicitly stated in dispensationalism, rather they are inferred and understood to be logical steps in the general framework.

  \*\* This point was not part of the Darby's original framework, it was introduced by later dispensationalist theologians and it is now considered part of mainstream dispensationalism.

Most Christian traditions interpret the "millennium" symbolically.

Dispensationalists insist it will be a literal, geopolitical reality.

This sequence is often visualized as a three-act drama:

- **Act 1**: Setup:- Israel's return, Rapture, rise of Antichrist
- **Act 2**: Escalation:- Temple desecration, judgments intensify
- **Act 3**: Resolution:-Christ's return, Satan bound, final judgment

To help readers visualize the theological framework discussed above, the following timeline illustrates the progression of dispensations and the prophetic milestones dispensationalists believe must unfold before the final era.

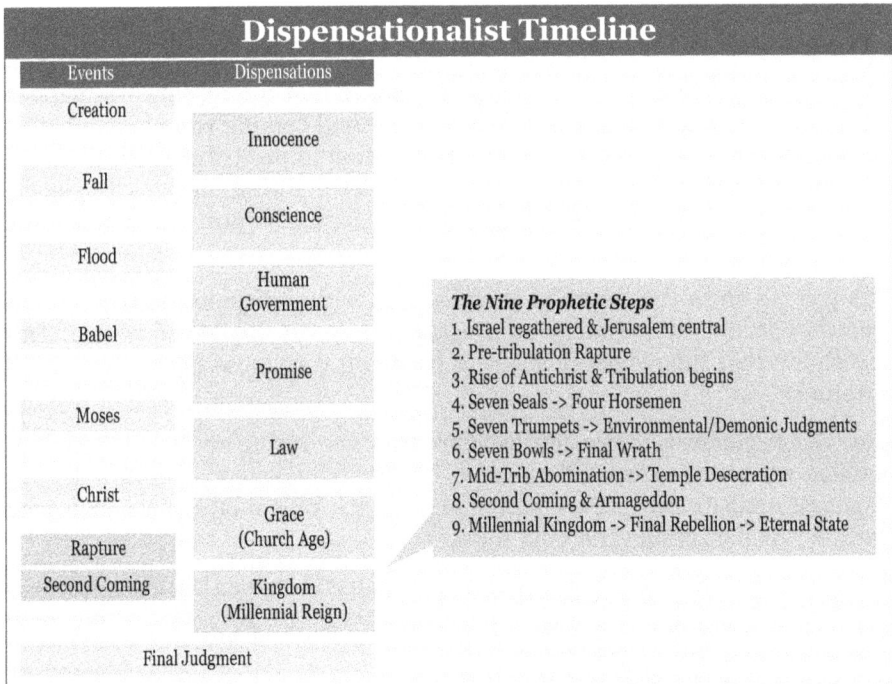

## Dispensationalist Timeline

| Events | Dispensations | |
|---|---|---|
| Creation | | |
| | Innocence | |
| Fall | | |
| | Conscience | |
| Flood | | |
| | Human Government | **The Nine Prophetic Steps** |
| Babel | | 1. Israel regathered & Jerusalem central |
| | Promise | 2. Pre-tribulation Rapture |
| | | 3. Rise of Antichrist & Tribulation begins |
| Moses | | 4. Seven Seals -> Four Horsemen |
| | Law | 5. Seven Trumpets -> Environmental/Demonic Judgments |
| | | 6. Seven Bowls -> Final Wrath |
| Christ | | 7. Mid-Trib Abomination -> Temple Desecration |
| | Grace (Church Age) | 8. Second Coming & Armageddon |
| Rapture | | 9. Millennial Kingdom -> Final Rebellion -> Eternal State |
| Second Coming | Kingdom (Millennial Reign) | |
| Final Judgment | | |

*Figure 1: Dispensational Timeline and Prophetic Roadmap*

From 1830 onward, Darby's dispensationalism became more than a theological system, it was a strategic worldview. It offered believers a structured lens through which to interpret scripture, history, and current events. It positioned Israel as the centerpiece of divine prophecy and gave Christians a role in preparing the world for the Second Coming.

This theology would become the engine behind Christian Zionism, transforming belief into action and prophecy into policy.

Having explained what the dispensationalist belief system is, it is important to highlight that since its invention almost 2 centuries ago, and primarily due to its interpretive nature, dispensationalism has been open to many different interpretations that developed into a few strands or variations within the concepts that Darby laid out and taught.

## Variations Within Dispensationalism

Dispensationalism is not monolithic. It includes Classical, Revised, and Progressive (Modern) streams. These differ in views on prophetic chronology, the relationship between Israel and the Church, and the nature of the Kingdom of God. Some even dispute the number of dispensations. Others disagree on the order of the nine prophetic steps and on the steps themselves. However, most dispensationalists affirm a **pre-tribulation, premillennial** outline (Blaising & Bock, 1993):

- **Pre-tribulation**: The Church is raptured **before** a seven-year Tribulation.

- **Premillennial**: Christ returns visibly **and then** reigns on Earth.

This means that most dispensationalists believe that the rapture will happen before the Tribulation begins, and that the second coming will happen before the Kingdom on earth is established. In addition to pre-tribulation, there are also mid-tribulation, and post-tribulation views within dispensationalism. Similarly, in addition to pre-millennial, there are also post- millennial, and Amillennial beliefs.

This goes to show that there is no consensus within dispensationalist circles even on concepts that should be considered core to this belief system. This also shows that this whole theology is based on very loose interpretations of scripture.

It is these differences that made it so hard from me during my research journey to fully wrap my head around this topic. However, it is safe to assume that most dispensationalists are pre-tribulational and pre-millennial which align with Darby's 7 dispensations and nine steps.

Another important distinction to point out, is that one between Dispensationalists and Christian Zionists.

## Passive Observers vs. Active Agents: Dispensationalists vs. Christian Zionists

While both dispensationalists and Christian Zionists believe in the nine prophetic steps, they differ in their roles:

- **Dispensationalists** see themselves as passive observers. God sets the timeline; their role is to remain faithful and watchful (Acts 1:7).

- **Christian Zionists** see themselves as active agents. They believe it is their divine duty to help implement the plan, supporting Israel, rebuilding the temple, and influencing U.S. foreign policy.

This distinction explains why Christian Zionists are politically mobilized, financially invested, and emotionally committed to Israeli state policies, even when those policies conflict with human rights or international law.

## Theology as Strategy

In mainstream dispensational thought, especially the pre-tribulation, premillennial variety, the Second Coming is not something believers can "trigger." The timing is set by God alone (Acts 1:7). However, many dispensational teachers emphasize present-day responsibilities that align with God's purposes:

- **Evangelism and discipleship** – Preparing people before the Rapture (Matthew 28:19–20)
- **Doctrinal faithfulness** – Resisting apostasy (2 Timothy 4:2–5)
- **Support for Israel** – Advocating for the Jewish people and the modern state of Israel (Genesis 12:3)
- **Watchfulness** –Living in readiness for Christ's imminent return

By contrast, Christian Zionists treat dispensationalism not just as a belief system, but as a call to action. The nine steps are not abstract predictions; they are tasks to be completed. This sense of divine duty drives support for Israel, advocacy for temple reconstruction, and political engagement across the globe.

Although mainstream dispensationalists often describe themselves as passive observers of a divine plan, their responses to world events suggest otherwise. In practice, they tend to embrace and celebrate developments that appear to align with their prophetic expectations, such as the expansion of Israeli territory or the recognition of Jerusalem as Israel's capital. Conversely, they are quick to reject or condemn any political or diplomatic efforts that contradict their interpretation of biblical prophecy, including peace initiatives that involve territorial compromise.

Their theological framework may not call for direct action, but it powerfully shapes how they interpret, support, or resist real-world events.

Understanding dispensationalism is essential to understanding Christian Zionism. It is the engine behind the movement, the theology that turns belief into strategy, and prophecy into policy.

As we will examine later in this book, this line between dispensationalists and Christian Zionists gets blurred because this theological posture has had profound political consequences, especially in 19th and 20th century Great Brittin and the United States until the present, where dispensationalist beliefs have deeply influenced public opinion, voting behavior, and foreign policy.

Darby's dispensationalist theology did not remain confined to academic circles or theological debates. It found fertile ground in a new religious movement, the Brethren, who not only embraced his prophetic framework but also developed a strategic infrastructure to disseminate it. In the next chapter, we explore how this small but influential group transformed Darby's ideas into a global mission.

# Part II
# Christian Zionism Takes Shape

# Chapter 5
## The Brethren Movement and Its Secretive Nature

With the theological framework of dispensationalism firmly established by **John Nelson Darby**, the next chapter in the story of Christian Zionism unfolds through a movement that quietly but strategically carried these ideas into the world: the **Brethren Movement**, often referred to as the **Plymouth Brethren**.

Though small in number, the Brethren were highly disciplined, deeply committed to their prophetic mission, and remarkably effective in spreading Darby's theology. Their influence extended far beyond their modest public profile, shaping religious communities, political leaders, and even Jewish thinkers. Their practices and organizational style bore striking similarities to secret societies, operating with discretion, exclusivity, and long-term strategic vision.

## Origins and Philosophy of the Brethren

The Brethren Movement began in **Dublin in the late 1820s**, with Darby as one of its most prominent founders. Disillusioned with the institutional Church of Ireland, Darby and others sought to return to what they considered the purity of early Christianity, free from denominational hierarchy, clerical authority, and ritualistic tradition (Weber, 2004).

The movement emphasized three core principles:

- **Biblical literalism**: Scripture was to be interpreted as the direct and unambiguous word of God.

- **Separation from the world**: Members were encouraged to live apart from secular society and politics.

- **Prophetic urgency**: The Second Coming of Christ was imminent, and believers had a role in preparing for it.

Worship was simple, often held in homes or rented halls. Leadership was informal, and gatherings were autonomous. Yet despite this outward simplicity, the Brethren developed a tightly controlled internal culture.

## Secrecy and Exclusivity

The Brethren's rejection of denominationalism did not translate into openness. In fact, the movement became known for its **insularity and secrecy**. Meetings were closed to outsiders, doctrinal conformity was strictly enforced, and dissent was often met with exclusion.

Some scholars have drawn parallels between the Brethren and **Freemasonry**, noting similarities such as:

- Hierarchical influence without formal titles

- Use of coded theological language

- Emphasis on hidden knowledge and divine mysteries

- Strategic networking across religious and political domains

While the Brethren did not adopt the rituals or symbols of Freemasonry, their organizational style and long-term planning suggest a shared ethos of quiet influence (Marsden, 1980).

## A Three-Pronged Strategy: Belief, Politics, and Influence

The Brethren Movement operated on **three simultaneous fronts**, each designed to advance dispensationalist theology and prepare the world for the final dispensation.

### 1. Evangelical Outreach

The first front was **recruitment and propagation of belief**. Brethren missionaries and teachers spread dispensationalist doctrine across Europe and North America, often targeting Protestant communities already receptive to apocalyptic themes. Darby's writings, sermons, and travels helped establish a network of dispensationalist churches and study groups (Mangum & Sweetnam, 2009).

These communities became incubators for Christian Zionist thought, reinforcing the idea that Jewish restoration to Palestine was a divine necessity. The Brethren's emphasis on prophecy and literal interpretation made them particularly effective in shaping eschatological discourse.

### 2. Political Lobbying

The second front was **political engagement**. Brethren leaders and sympathizers sought to influence government policy, especially in Britain, to support the establishment of a Jewish homeland in Palestine. This was not driven by humanitarian concern for the Jews; it was a theological imperative.

Figures like Lord Shaftesbury, a devout evangelical and supporter of dispensationalism, worked closely with politicians such as Lord Palmerston to promote British involvement in Jewish resettlement. Shaftesbury famously popularized the phrase, "*a land without a people for a people without a land,*" encapsulating the Christian Zionist vision of Jewish restoration (Lewis, 2010).

This political strategy was subtle but effective. By embedding theological goals within diplomatic language, the Brethren and their allies were able to shape foreign policy without overt religious rhetoric.

### 3. Engagement with Jewish Communities

The third front was **direct engagement with Jews in Europe** to encourage them to leave Europe and resettle in Palestine; because if the Jews do not want to establish a homeland in Palestine, the whole project of ushering in the Second Coming would fall apart. Brethren missionaries, including Rev. William Hechler, traveled across the continent seeking Jews who might be receptive to the idea of returning to Palestine. Hechler believed that Jewish restoration was essential for the Second Coming and saw himself as a facilitator of prophecy (Ariel, 2013).

At the time, most Jewish communities, both Orthodox and Reform, rejected the idea of resettlement in Palestine. The notion was seen as impractical, dangerous, and theologically unsound. Yet Hechler persisted, eventually connecting with Theodor Herzl, the father of modern Jewish Zionism. Their alliance would prove pivotal in transforming Christian Zionist aspirations into political reality.

## The Brethren's Legacy and Influence

The Brethren Movement's influence extended far beyond its numbers. Through **strategic outreach, political lobbying, and theological innovation**, it laid the groundwork for a global Christian Zionist movement. Its emphasis on secrecy, prophecy, and divine mission created a culture of quiet determination, one that continues to shape evangelical thought and foreign policy to this day.

While the Brethren may not have operated with the formal structure of Freemasonry, their impact was no less profound. They built a network of believers who saw themselves as agents of divine history, working behind the scenes to fulfill prophecy and prepare the world for Christ's return.

Their theological vision found powerful allies in the political realm. Evangelical leaders like Lord Shaftesbury used their influence to shape British foreign policy, advocating for Jewish restoration not as a matter of diplomacy, but as a fulfillment of biblical prophecy.

While the Brethren operated largely in religious and missionary circles, their theological vision soon found allies in the political realm. Evangelical statesmen like Lord Shaftesbury and Lord Palmerston would take up the mantle, translating prophecy into policy and theology into imperial strategy. The next chapter explores how Christian Zionism moved from the pulpit to Parliament.

# Chapter 6
## The Political Push
## Lord Shaftesbury and Lord Palmerston

As dispensationalist theology gained traction through the **Brethren Movement**, its influence began to seep into the political corridors of **19th-century Britain**. The belief that Jewish restoration to Palestine was a prerequisite for the Second Coming of Christ was no longer confined to religious gatherings, it became a strategic objective for evangelical statesmen. Among the most influential figures in this transformation were **Lord Shaftesbury** and **Lord Palmerston**, whose partnership helped turn Christian Zionist theology into British foreign policy.

Before Lord Shaftesbury's political influence is explored, it's essential to understand the theological current he represented. Some evangelicals in the early 19th century held beliefs that would later be recognized as **proto-Christian Zionism**.

**Proto-Christian Zionism** refers to early theological views, predating formal dispensationalism, that saw the restoration of Jews to Palestine as a fulfillment of biblical prophecy. These beliefs were not yet systematized into a full eschatological framework, but they laid the ideological groundwork for later Christian Zionist activism.

Figures like Alexander Keith and organizations such as the London Society for Promoting Christianity Amongst the Jews promoted Jewish resettlement in Palestine not out of humanitarian concern, but as a prophetic necessity. Shaftesbury would become one of the most influential political voices to carry these theological convictions into the realm of government policy.

## Lord Shaftesbury: Proto-Christian Zionist Statesman and Prophetic Strategist

**Anthony Ashley-Cooper, the 7th Earl of Shaftesbury (1801–1885)**, was one of the most prominent evangelical politicians of his time. Known for his humanitarian reforms, such as improving labor conditions and mental health care, Shaftesbury was also deeply committed to **restorational beliefs**. Although he did not believe in the newly invented dispensationalist theology, he was a proto-Christian Zionist in his world view. He believed that the Jews must return to Palestine to fulfill biblical prophecy and usher in the second coming (Lewis, 2010).

Lord Shaftesbury, (1801–1885)

Shaftesbury's religious convictions were not passive beliefs; they were political motivators. He used his position in Parliament and his influence in elite circles to advocate for Jewish resettlement in Palestine. In 1840, he famously wrote in the *Quarterly Review* that "the soil and climate of Palestine are admirably adapted to the growth of the produce peculiar to the country," arguing that Jewish restoration was both spiritually necessary and economically viable (Lewis, 2010, p. 45).

His most enduring contribution to Christian Zionist rhetoric was the phrase:

> *"We have there a land teeming with fertility and rich in history,*
> *but almost without an inhabitant — a country without a people,*
> *and look! scattered over the world, a people without a country."*

This slogan, though historically inaccurate, became a powerful tool in framing Jewish resettlement as both benevolent and prophetic. It erased the presence of native Palestinians and positioned the Jews as rightful inheritors of a supposedly vacant land, an idea that would later be echoed in Zionist discourse (Masalha, 2012). The phrase "a land without a people for a people without a land," was first coined by Christian Restorationists like Alexander Keith in the 1840s and later used by Shaftesbury in lobbying efforts with the British government, decades before there were any Jewish aspirations to resettle in Palestine. In his 1853 letter to Prime Minister Aberdeen and his 1854 diary entry, Shaftesbury described Palestine as *"a country without a nation; and God now, in His wisdom and mercy, directs us to a nation without a country."*

Shaftesbury's religious motivations were further institutionalized through his presidency of the **London Society for Promoting Christianity Amongst the Jews**, an evangelical group that saw Jewish restoration as a divine imperative.

## Lord Palmerston: Diplomatic Enabler of Prophetic Policy

**Henry John Temple, 3rd Viscount Palmerston (1784–1865)**, served as British Foreign Secretary and later Prime Minister. Though not an evangelical himself, Palmerston was receptive to Shaftesbury's ideas and recognized the strategic value of supporting Jewish resettlement in Palestine. His motivations were geopolitical: the Ottoman Empire was weakening, and Britain sought to expand its influence in the Middle East. Supporting Jewish restoration aligned with both evangelical prophecy and imperial strategy.

Lord Palmerston, (1784-1865)

Palmerston's decision was not made in isolation. He was married to Emily Lamb, the widowed mother-in-law of Shaftesbury. This familial connection gave Shaftesbury unique access to Palmerston's ear. In one diary entry, Shaftesbury recounts a dinner he hosted for Palmerston and his mother-in-law. After the meal, the two men sat alone, and Shaftesbury made his case: that it would be in Britain's strategic interest to support the establishment of a Jewish homeland in Palestine. He argued that such a state, loyal to Britain, would help further weaken the Ottoman Empire and secure British influence in the region. Palmerston, though not a believer himself, was reportedly convinced by the political and economic logic, and, as Shaftesbury noted in his diary, "was moved to fulfill God's will and prophecy" (Lewis, 2010; Weber, 2004).

In 1840, Palmerston instructed the British ambassador in Constantinople to encourage the Ottoman authorities to allow Jews to settle in Palestine. This marked one of the earliest instances of Christian Zionist theology directly shaping imperial policy, not for Jewish interests, but to fulfill Christian prophecy and secure British influence (Lewis, 2010).

*Emily Lamb (1787-1869)*

## The Evangelical-Political Alliance

The partnership between **Shaftesbury and Palmerston** exemplifies the **evangelical–political alliance** that drove early Christian Zionist efforts. Shaftesbury provided the theological rationale, rooted in dispensationalist prophecy, while Palmerston translated that vision into diplomatic action.

This alliance was not isolated. It reflected a broader trend in 19th-century Britain, where evangelical movements increasingly influenced public policy. Missionary societies, Bible societies, and prophetic conferences created a climate in which religious goals were pursued through political means (Weber, 2004).

Even scientific institutions were drawn into this theological orbit. For example, Shaftesbury's 1875 speech at a **Palestine Exploration Fund (PEF)** meeting emphasized biblical motivations behind archaeological research in the Holy Land.

The result was a subtle but powerful shift: Jewish restoration was no longer just a religious hope, it became a strategic objective of the British Empire.

## Legacy and Impact

The efforts of **Shaftesbury and Palmerston** laid the groundwork for future British support of Zionism. Their actions helped normalize the idea that Jewish resettlement in Palestine was both desirable and inevitable.

This ideological foundation would later influence the **Balfour Declaration of 1917**, in which Britain formally endorsed the establishment of a Jewish homeland in Palestine.

Arthur James Balfour, Britain's Foreign Secretary who authored the declaration, was influenced by Christian Restorationist ideas. Balfour, a Scottish

*Lord Balfour (1848, 1930)*

Presbyterian, believed in the "restoration of the Jews" as part of biblical prophecy. Prime Minister David Lloyd George also expressed sympathy for Zionism rooted in his biblical upbringing. Notably, Shaftesbury was Balfour's grand-uncle by marriage, and his legacy lived on in British policy circles.

However, it's important to note that the Balfour Declaration was also driven by wartime strategy, particularly Britain's desire to gain Jewish support in Russia and the United States during World War I. Christian Zionist influence was one pillar among several, not the sole driver.

*D. Lloyd George (1863-1945)*

## Interwar Period and the British Mandate: Theology Meets Military Strategy

While the Balfour Declaration marked a formal endorsement of Jewish restoration, the British Mandate (1920–1948) revealed the tensions between imperial strategy and prophetic theology. Britain's policy was pulled between its commitment to the Balfour Declaration and growing Arab opposition. Yet Christian Zionist influence did not wane, it evolved.

One of the most striking examples was **Orde Wingate**, a British army officer stationed in Palestine during the late 1930s. Wingate was a zealous Christian Zionist who believed the Jewish people were fulfilling biblical prophecy. A devoted Bible reader, he saw his military mission as a spiritual calling. He helped train Jewish militias and was instrumental in forming the **Special Night Squads** with the **Haganah** during the **Arab Revolt (1936–1939)**.

Wingate's actions were not merely tactical, they were theological. He believed that supporting Jewish military strength was part of God's plan. His legacy would later influence Israeli military doctrine and reinforce the idea that prophecy could be fulfilled through force. While Wingate's story may be beyond the scope of this overview, it exemplifies how Christian Zionism shaped not only policy but battlefield strategy.

*Orde Wingate (1903-1944)*

As Shaftesbury and Palmerston laid the political groundwork for Christian Zionism, another figure emerged who would connect these theological ambitions with the nascent Jewish Zionist movement. Rev. William Hechler, a devout Christian Zionist with royal connections, would become the matchmaker between prophecy and politics. His story begins in Vienna.

In the next chapter, we will explore Hechler's background, his connection with Theodor Herzl, and how their unlikely alliance helped transform Christian Zionist theology into the political reality of Jewish Zionism.

# Chapter 7
## Rev. William Hechler
## The Matchmaker of Zionism

While **Christian Zionist** theology had already begun influencing British policy through figures like **Lord Shaftesbury** and **Lord Palmerston**, its full realization required a bridge to the emerging Jewish Zionist movement. That bridge was built by **Rev. William Hechler**, a British clergyman of German descent whose religious convictions and diplomatic connections helped elevate **Theodor Herzl** from a journalist to a statesman, and catalyzed the birth of modern Zionism.

## William Hechler: German Roots and Royal Connections

**Rev. William Hechler (1845–1931)** was born in India to a British missionary family but had **German ancestry** and strong ties to the German royal court. He served as **chaplain to the British Embassy in Vienna** and had previously tutored the children of **Frederick, Grand Duke of Baden**, making him well-connected within German aristocracy (Ariel, 2013).

His education in both England and Germany, along with his linguistic proficiency in Hebrew and Arabic, further deepened his engagement with Jewish history and theology (Hechler, 2009).

*William Hechler, (1845-1931)*

Hechler was a devout Christian Zionist, deeply influenced by dispensationalist theology. He believed that the restoration of the Jews to Palestine was a prerequisite for the Second Coming of Christ. He meticulously calculated prophetic timelines and believed that the time for Jewish return had arrived.

Hechler's German connections gave him access to influential figures, including **Kaiser Wilhelm II**, and his diplomatic role positioned him to act as a bridge between Christian Zionist aspirations and Jewish political efforts.

*Fredrick I (1826-1907)*

In his role as Metropolitan Secretary of the Church Pastoral Aid Society, Hechler traveled across Europe in 1882 to assess the conditions of Jewish communities, particularly in Russia, where he witnessed the aftermath of violent pogroms. During this journey, he met proto-Zionist Leon Pinsker in Odessa and recognized the growing aspirations for Jewish national revival among Eastern European Jews (Klinger, 2010).

*Wilhelm II (1859-1918)*

Hechler's Restorationist convictions led him to believe that the return of Jews to Palestine was a necessary precursor to the Second Coming of Christ. Unlike many of his contemporaries, he did not see Jewish conversion to Christianity as a prerequisite for this return. In 1884, he published *The Restoration of the Jews to Palestine*, advocating for Jewish resettlement in the Holy Land as a divine imperative and Christian duty (Hechler, 2009).

Hechler also attempted to influence political leaders. Two years earlier, while in Istanbul, he tried, unsuccessfully, to deliver a letter from Queen Victoria to the Sultan of the Ottoman Empire, urging the restoration of Jews to Palestine. The British Ambassador to Istanbul refused to deliver the letter on the basis that it would bypass official diplomatic channels and that it would be perceived by the Sultan as further evidence of foreign interference. Nonetheless, Hechler's efforts reflected a blend of religious conviction and political activism aimed at legitimizing Jewish national aspirations (Klinger, 2010).

Privately, Hechler immersed himself in biblical prophecy, constructing timelines and even a scale model of the Jewish Temple. He predicted that a significant event related to Jewish restoration would occur around 1897–1898, a forecast that coincided with the publication of Herzl's *Der Judenstaat* and their eventual meeting (Hechler, 2009).

## Theodor Herzl: Background and Early Worldview

**Theodor Herzl** (1860–1904) was born in Budapest to a secular Jewish family that had embraced Enlightenment ideals. He was educated in law and literature, and later became a journalist and playwright. Herzl's early worldview was shaped by the liberal optimism of 19th-century Europe, where assimilation seemed possible and nationalism was on the rise (Laqueur, 2003).

As a correspondent for the Viennese newspaper *Neue Freie Presse*, Herzl covered political and cultural events across Europe. He initially believed that antisemitism could be overcome through integration and education. At one point, he even proposed mass conversion of Jews to Christianity as a solution to antisemitic hostility, a reflection of his early detachment from Jewish religious identity (Patai, 1975).

*Theodor Herzl (1860-1904)*

Herzl's transformation from assimilationist to Zionist was not gradual, it was triggered by a single, seismic event.

## The Dreyfus Affair: A Turning Point

In 1894, **Captain Alfred Dreyfus**, a Jewish officer in the French army, was falsely accused of treason and sentenced to life imprisonment. The trial was marked by overt antisemitism, and the public reaction revealed deep-rooted hostility toward Jews, even in supposedly liberal France.

Herzl was in Paris covering the trial. He witnessed mobs shouting "Death to the Jews!" and saw how fragile Jewish acceptance truly was. The Dreyfus Affair shattered his belief in assimilation and convinced him that Jews would never be safe in Europe without a state of their own (Laqueur, 2003; Weber, 2004).

This realization propelled Herzl to write a book that would become the foundational text of modern Zionism.

*Alfred Dreyfus (1859-1935)*

## Der Judenstaat: Vision and Proposals

Published in 1896, *Der Judenstaat* (*The Jewish State*) laid out Herzl's vision for a sovereign Jewish homeland. The book was not religious, it was political. Herzl argued that antisemitism was a permanent feature of European society and that the only solution was the establishment of a Jewish state through organized migration and international diplomacy (Herzl, 1896/1988).

Key proposals in the book included:

- The creation of a **Jewish Company** to manage land acquisition and infrastructure.
- A phased migration of Jews, beginning with the poor and working class.
- A modern, secular state governed by law and equality, not by religious authority.
- **Location options**: Herzl proposed either **Palestine** or **Argentina** as potential sites, based on feasibility and international support.

The book was met with mixed reactions:

- **Orthodox Jews** rejected it, believing that only the Messiah could restore Israel.
- **Reformist Jews** opposed it, fearing it would undermine their efforts to integrate into European society.
- **Eastern European Jews**, facing pogroms and persecution, were more receptive, and Herzl's ideas gained traction among them (Laqueur, 2003; Ariel, 2013).

Herzl's proposals were bold, pragmatic, and secular, but they resonated with Christian Zionists for entirely different reasons.

## The Hechler–Herzl Connection

Reverend William Hechler – at the time happened to be serving as the chaplain of the British Embassy in Vienna - first encountered Theodor Herzl's ideas in early March 1896 when he discovered a copy of *Der Judenstaat* at a Viennese bookstall. The book, which proposed the establishment of a Jewish state as a solution to antisemitism, resonated deeply with Hechler's Restorationist beliefs and prophetic calculations, which had predicted a Jewish return to Palestine around 1897–1898 (Hechler, 2009).

On **March 10, 1896**, Hechler visited Herzl for the first time. Herzl described him in his diary as *"a likeable, sensitive man with the long grey beard of a prophet,"* noting that Hechler viewed the Zionist movement as a "prophetic crisis" he had anticipated based on biblical prophecy (Lowenthal, 1978). Hechler believed Herzl's movement was divinely ordained and immediately sought to support it by leveraging his connections to European royalty, particularly the German court.

Their second meeting occurred just days later, when Herzl visited Hechler's home. Herzl was struck by Hechler's eccentric yet passionate dedication: his apartment was filled with Bibles, maps of Palestine, and a scale model of the Jewish Temple. Hechler showed Herzl a large military map of Palestine and explained his vision for the future Jewish state, even pointing out where the new Temple should be built, at Bethel, the geographic center of the land (Lowenthal, 1978).

Despite finding Hechler somewhat naïve and overly visionary, Herzl recognized his strategic value. Hechler had access to the German aristocracy, including the Grand Duke of Baden and Kaiser Wilhelm II. Herzl confided in Hechler that he needed public recognition from a European ruler to gain credibility among Jews and political leaders. Hechler responded enthusiastically, offering to travel to Berlin to arrange introductions and requesting travel expenses, which Herzl agreed to provide (Lowenthal, 1978).

Hechler's efforts soon bore fruit. In April 1896, he arranged for Herzl to meet the Grand Duke of Baden, who was impressed both by Hechler's prophetic charts and Herzl's political vision. This meeting marked the first time Herzl's ideas were seriously considered by European royalty, and it was a pivotal step in legitimizing the Zionist movement (Klinger, 2010).

Hechler's theological motives differed sharply from Herzl's secular vision, yet their alliance proved vital.

## Hechler's Contributions to Herzl and the Zionist Movement

Reverend William Hechler played a pivotal role in legitimizing and advancing Theodor Herzl's Zionist vision, acting as a bridge between Christian Restorationist thought and emerging Jewish political Zionism. His contributions were multifaceted, spanning theological support, political networking, and personal advocacy.

### 1. Theological and Moral Support

Hechler's Restorationist beliefs aligned closely with Herzl's political goals.

He believed that the return of Jews to Palestine was a fulfillment of biblical prophecy and a necessary step toward the Second Coming of Christ. Unlike many Christian Zionists of his time, Hechler did not insist on Jewish conversion to Christianity, instead advocating for Jewish self-determination as a divine imperative (Hechler, 2009). His theological endorsement gave Herzl's secular vision a broader religious resonance, particularly among Christian audiences.

## 2. Political Legitimization and Access to Royalty

One of Hechler's most significant contributions was his ability to **open doors to European royalty**. Drawing on his past as tutor to the children of Frederick I, Grand Duke of Baden, and his connections to Kaiser Wilhelm II, Hechler arranged Herzl's first audience with the Grand Duke in April 1896.

Hechler later facilitated Herzl's introduction to the German Kaiser during Wilhelm II's 1898 visit to Palestine. Although the Kaiser ultimately withdrew his support, the public meeting between Herzl and the German monarch was a symbolic victory, signaling that Zionism had gained a foothold in European diplomacy (Klinger, 2010).

## 3. Hechler's Role in British Introductions

Herzl recognized the strategic importance of British support for Zionism and asked Hechler to help him gain access to the British royal court. At the time, the British Empire was one of the world's superpowers that has colonized vast territories around the world. Endorsing and supporting Herzl's vision would have been essential. However, Hechler's influence in Britain had waned by that time, and he was unable to secure the same level of access he had achieved in Germany.

Although Hechler's efforts in Britain did not yield immediate political results, they were significant for several reasons:

- **Symbolic Legitimacy**: His attempts to involve the British monarchy underscored the Zionist movement's desire for international recognition and support from major powers.
- **Christian Zionist Advocacy**: Hechler's actions helped frame Zionism not only as a Jewish national movement but also as a cause with Christian theological backing, which appealed to certain segments of British society.
- **Foundation for Future Support**: While Hechler himself did not succeed in securing British political backing, his early advocacy laid the groundwork for later British involvement, culminating in the Balfour Declaration of 1917.

## 4. Advocacy and Public Relations

Hechler tirelessly promoted Herzl's cause in Christian and diplomatic circles. He attended multiple Zionist Congresses as Herzl's aide and was often described as the first Christian Zionist to be formally involved in the movement. He wrote letters, gave speeches, and used his clerical position to advocate for Jewish restoration to Palestine (Lowenthal, 1978).

## 5. Personal Loyalty and Emotional Support

Beyond his political and theological contributions, Hechler was a steadfast companion to Herzl. He remained by Herzl's side during his final days and recorded his last words: "Greet Palestine for me. I gave my heart's blood for my people" (Klinger, 2010). Herzl, in turn, asked that the Zionist movement remember and honor Hechler for his unwavering support.

Hechler's support was far more than symbolic, it was strategically transformative. He provided Herzl with access to influential circles, conferred legitimacy on his ideas, and framed Herzl's vision within a theological narrative that resonated deeply with Christian audiences. In just over a year from their first meeting, Herzl rose from relative obscurity to being received as a statesman by European leaders. His proposal, once dismissed across the Jewish ideological spectrum in Europe, had become a subject of serious debate, not only among Jews, but also within powerful non-Jewish circles who now saw it as politically and diplomatically relevant.

## The First Zionist Congress: A Shared Milestone

In **1897**, Herzl convened the **First Zionist Congress** in Basel, Switzerland. The event marked the formal beginning of the **Jewish Zionist movement**. While Herzl provided the political framework, Hechler's theological and diplomatic groundwork helped make it possible.

Christian Zionists saw the Congress as a prophetic milestone. Hechler believed it was a sign that the end times were near and that the restoration of Israel was underway. Herzl, for his part, understood the value of Christian support, even if he did not share its eschatological goals.

## A Strategic Alliance with Divergent Goals

The Hechler–Herzl partnership exemplifies the complex relationship between Christian and Jewish Zionism. While both movements sought the establishment of a Jewish homeland in Palestine, their motivations were fundamentally different:

- **Jewish Zionists** aimed to create a safe haven and national revival.
- **Christian Zionists** saw Jewish restoration as a step toward apocalyptic fulfillment and the return of Christ.

This divergence would later lead to tensions, but in the late 19th century, it created a powerful alliance. Hechler's role as matchmaker was pivotal, he connected prophecy with politics, theology with diplomacy, and belief with strategy.

While Christian Zionism and Jewish Zionism both supported the establishment of a Jewish homeland in Palestine, their motivations were fundamentally different. One was driven by prophecy, the other by survival. The following infographic illustrates the theological, political, and cultural contrasts between these two movements, revealing how a shared destination masked radically different visions for its purpose and future.

# One Homeland, Two Theologies: The Christian–Jewish Zionist Divide

| CHRISTIAN ZIONISM | JEWISH ZIONISM |
|---|---|
| **Theological Motivation**<br>Fulfillment of biblical prophecy and the Second Coming of Christ | **Political Motivation**<br>Establishment of a safe, sovereign homeland for Jews |
| **Key Belief**<br>Jews must return to Palestine to trigger end-times events | **Key Belief**<br>Jews have a historical and cultural right to self-determination |
| **Ultimate Goal**<br>Rebuilding the Temple, rise of the Antichrist, return of Jesus | **Ultimate Goal**<br>National revival, security, and cultural preservation |
| **View of Jews**<br>Instruments in a divine plan; eventual conversion or destruction | **View of Christians**<br>Allies of convenience; disagree on the outcome, but are willing to take financial, military, political, and diplomatic support |
| **Insistence on Location**<br>Palestine only — to fulfill prophecy | **Pragmatic on Location**<br>Initially considered Argentina, Uganda, etc. |
| **Support Base**<br>Evangelical Christians, especially in the U.S. | **Support Base**<br>Secular and religious Jews worldwide |
| **Endgame**<br>Apocalyptic fulfillment, not coexistence | **Endgame**<br>Jewish survival and supremacy |

*Figure 2: Christian vs. Jewish Zionism*

While both movements supported the establishment of a Jewish homeland in Palestine, their motivations diverged sharply. This infographic contrasts their theological foundations, political goals, and long-term visions.

## It was the Christian Zionists that insisted on Palestine

It is critical to emphasize that Christian Zionists, particularly British evangelicals, were strongly committed to the idea that the Jewish homeland must be in Palestine, and that their support for Zionism was conditional on this location.

- **Rev. William Hechler**, was deeply committed to the idea that **Palestine** was the only acceptable location for the Jewish state. He believed this was necessary to fulfill biblical prophecy. When Theodor Herzl proposed alternative locations such as **Argentina** in *Der Judenstaat*, Hechler **insisted on Palestine** and actively steered Herzl toward that goal (Ariel, 2013; Lewis, 2010).
- During the **Uganda Proposal** debate in 1903, many Christian Zionists

**opposed the idea** of a Jewish homeland anywhere other than Palestine. Their opposition was theological: only Palestine fulfilled the prophetic conditions for the Second Coming of Christ (Weber, 2004).

- **Lord Shaftesbury**, decades earlier, had already framed Jewish restoration to **Palestine** as a divine imperative. The infamous phrase that erased the existence of the Palestinian people, "a land without a people for a people without a land", was specifically about Palestine, and his lobbying efforts were focused on that region (Lewis, 2010).

- In Herzl's own writings and correspondence, he acknowledged that **Christian support was strongest when Palestine was the destination**. While he was pragmatic about location, he understood that Christian Zionists viewed Palestine as non-negotiable (Laqueur, 2003).

Hechler helped bridge Christian Zionist theology with Jewish political aspirations. However, the movement's greatest expansion occurred across the Atlantic. In the United States, dispensationalism found fertile ground in evangelical churches, revivalist movements, and popular media.

## The American Parallel: Blackstone's Memorials and Brandeis

While Hechler was building bridges in Europe, a parallel movement was emerging in the United States. In 1891, American Christian Zionist William E. Blackstone submitted a petition to President Benjamin Harrison urging the U.S. to support the return of Jews to Palestine. The petition was signed by over 400 prominent Americans, including John D. Rockefeller, J.P. Morgan, and future President William McKinley (Sandeen, 1970; Weber, 2004).

Although the petition did not result in immediate policy changes, it laid the groundwork for future support. In 1916, Justice Louis Brandeis rediscovered Blackstone's memorial and called him the "Father of Zionism," acknowledging that Blackstone's advocacy predated Herzl's political mobilization. Brandeis's endorsement helped elevate Blackstone's influence and connected American Christian Zionism to the broader Zionist movement (Ariel, 2013).

In May 1917, Blackstone, then 75 years old, submitted a second memorial (petition) to President Woodrow Wilson, urging support for a Jewish homeland. Wilson, a devout Presbyterian, was reportedly moved by the appeal. Historians suggest that Blackstone's petition helped solidify Wilson's favorable stance toward the **Balfour Declaration**, issued by Britain in November 1917 (Lewis, 2010).

*William Blackstone (1841-1935)*

## The Balfour Declaration: Promise and Contradiction

The **Balfour Declaration** was a letter from British Foreign Secretary Arthur James Balfour to Lord Rothschild, expressing support for the establishment of a "national home for the Jewish people" in Palestine. It included a caveat that "nothing shall be done which may prejudice the civil and religious rights of existing non-Jewish communities in Palestine."

This contradiction, promising a homeland while preserving the rights of the indigenous population, was never reconciled. The declaration was driven by multiple factors: Christian Zionist sympathies, wartime strategy, and Zionist lobbying. Balfour himself was influenced by Restorationist theology, and Prime Minister David Lloyd George later acknowledged his biblical upbringing as shaping his views on Zionism (Weber, 2004).

The declaration marked a turning point. It legitimized Zionist aspirations on the world stage and set the stage for British control of Palestine under the Mandate system. But it also sowed the seeds of conflict, as Palestinians opposed the declaration from the outset, recognizing its implications for their future.

While Hechler's efforts helped legitimize Zionism in Europe, the movement's greatest expansion would occur across the Atlantic. In the United States, dispensationalist theology found fertile ground in evangelical churches, revivalist movements, and popular media. The next chapter explores how Cyrus Scofield transformed Darby's framework into a distinctly American belief system.

# Part III

# The American Engine

# Chapter 8
## Cyrus Scofield and the Americanization of Dispensationalism

Chapter 8

The transatlantic journey of **dispensationalist theology** found its most potent expression not in the sermons of **John Nelson Darby**, but in the annotations of a man whose name would become synonymous with American evangelicalism: **Cyrus Ingerson Scofield**. While Darby laid the theological groundwork, it was Scofield who translated that framework into a format that would shape the religious imagination of millions across North America.

## Scofield's Background and Influence

**Cyrus I. Scofield (1843–1921)** was a man of contradictions. Born in Michigan and raised in Tennessee, he served in the Confederate Army during the American Civil War. After the war, he pursued a career in law and politics, eventually becoming U.S. District Attorney for Kansas. However, his early career was marred by scandal, including allegations of forgery, bribery, and abandonment of his family. These personal and professional failures culminated in what Scofield later described as a profound spiritual crisis, a turning point that led to his conversion to evangelical Christianity (Mangum & Sweetnam, 2009).

*Cyrus I. Scofield (1843-1921)*

Scofield had **no formal theological education**. Nevertheless, he began referring to himself as a **'Doctor of Divinity' (D.D.)**, a title that gave him an air of scholarly authority, despite the absence of any academic record. This self-styling was emblematic of Scofield's broader approach: authoritative, confident, and deeply committed to a literalist interpretation of scripture. This self-styled authority would later shape millions of minds through his annotated Bible.

Scofield was introduced to dispensationalism through the teachings of Darby and the Plymouth Brethren, particularly through the Niagara Bible Conference, a key hub for prophetic theology in the late 19th century (Sandeen, 1970). He quickly became one of Darby's most influential American disciples, though he never publicly credited Darby in his later work. Instead, Scofield took the core tenets of dispensationalism and repackaged them for an American audience, one hungry for clarity, certainty, and a roadmap to the end times.

## The Scofield Reference Bible

In 1909, Scofield published what would become his magnum opus: the **Scofield Reference Bible**. This was no ordinary Bible. It was a **King James Version embedded with Scofield's own commentary**, footnotes that appeared at the bottom of nearly every page, offering theological interpretation and cross-references that guided the reader's understanding of the text. These notes were not neutral; they were explicitly dispensationalist, interpreting both the Old and New Testaments through the lens of Darby's prophetic framework.

Scofield's contribution was revolutionary. For the first time, a Bible was published that not only presented the sacred text but also explained it, page by page, according to a specific theological system. His annotations outlined the seven dispensations of human history. They emphasized the literal fulfillment of prophecy and reinforced the idea that God's promises to Israel were eternal, distinct from those made to the Church.

In addition to the footnotes, the Scofield Reference Bible included maps, charts, and graphics, visual tools that helped readers trace the unfolding of biblical prophecy. These additions made the Bible not just a sacred text, but a study guide, a theological manual, and a prophetic blueprint.

The impact was immediate and profound. The Scofield Reference Bible became the go-to Bible for anyone in North America who wanted to study Christianity seriously. It was adopted by churches, seminaries, and Bible colleges across the United States and Canada. For many evangelicals, to read the Bible was to read it through Scofield's eyes.

## Impact on American Evangelical Theology

The **Scofield Reference Bible** did more than popularize dispensationalism, it **institutionalized** it. By embedding his commentary directly into the biblical text, Scofield blurred the line between scripture and interpretation. His notes were often read with the same reverence as the verses themselves, giving his theological views an authority that few commentators before or since have achieved.

This influence extended far beyond the pulpit. Scofield's Bible shaped the worldview of generations of American Christians, particularly in the South and Midwest. It provided a framework for understanding world events, interpreting history, and anticipating the future. The establishment of the state of Israel in 1948 was seen by many as a direct fulfillment of Scofield's prophetic roadmap, a validation of his theology and a confirmation of divine providence. This theological lens would later shape American attitudes toward Israel and the Middle East.

The Scofield Reference Bible did not merely popularize dispensationalist theology, it became the best-selling religious book in North America after the King James Bible itself (Mangum & Sweetnam, 2009). Its widespread adoption across churches, seminaries, and households meant that millions of Christians were exposed to a single interpretive lens, one that framed biblical prophecy as a literal roadmap to geopolitical events. Crucially, most readers were unaware that Scofield's annotations represented just one theological perspective among many. They were not taught that other Christian traditions, Catholic, Orthodox, and even many Protestant denominations, reject dispensationalism entirely. Instead, they were led to believe that this interpretation was the only true Christianity, and that all others were false or heretical. This doctrinal exclusivity was reinforced in everyday conversations, sermons, and cultural norms. I recall asking my colleague Clark if he was Catholic, and his sharp reply, "No man,

I'm Christian", revealed not just a denominational distinction, but a theological boundary. In his mind, Catholicism was not Christianity. Scofield's framework shaped a theological echo chamber. In this mindset, empathy for others, especially Palestinians, was often shut down by a belief system that sanctified suffering as prophecy fulfillment.

## The Prophetic Fulfillment and the Switch in the American Mind

But the impact of these events on the American public was not merely theological, it was emotional, even euphoric. The founding of Israel in 1948 was perceived by many evangelicals as a miraculous achievement against overwhelming odds. The fledgling state's survival and military success were interpreted not as political victories, but as divine interventions. When Israel triumphed again in the 1967 Six-Day War, seizing East Jerusalem, the West Bank, the Golan Heights, Gaza, and the Sinai Peninsula, many American Christians saw it as further proof that biblical prophecy was unfolding before their eyes.

These events galvanized Christian Zionist support for Israel. The victories were not just military, they were spiritual milestones. They reinforced the belief that the modern state of Israel was not only legitimate but sacred. The phrase "God will bless those who bless Israel, and curse those who curse Israel" (Genesis 12:3) became a theological cornerstone. It was repeated in sermons, printed on bumper stickers, and woven into the fabric of American Christian Zionist identity.

This belief system created a powerful moral shield around Israel. For many Christian Zionists, Israel's actions, no matter how controversial, are seen as part of God's plan, because they believe prophecy is being fulfilled. The occupation of Palestinian land, the displacement of families, the destruction of homes, and the repeated military campaigns were not seen as political or ethical issues. They were divine necessities. To question them was to question God's will.

This was the "switch" I encountered so often during my years in the United States. Conversations about Palestine would begin with curiosity or even empathy, but the moment Israel was mentioned, something changed. A mental barrier would rise. The suffering of Palestinians became irrelevant, even justified, because it was assumed to be part of a divine script. I could feel it happen in real time, a subtle but unmistakable shift in the conversation, as if a voice in their minds whispered, "Do not empathize further."

What many of these well-meaning Christians did not realize was that the prophecy they believed was being fulfilled was not divine at all. It was manmade. The theological framework that shaped their worldview was constructed by Darby, annotated by Scofield, and disseminated through pulpits and publishing houses, not handed down from heaven. The establishment of the state of Israel and its territorial expansion in 1967 were not the result of divine intervention, but of political maneuvering, military strategy, and a vast web of international deals and conspiracies, many of which were made at the expense of the Palestinian people.

Scofield's theological legacy did not remain confined to pulpits or seminaries, it permeated the cultural and political consciousness of American evangelicalism. His reference Bible became the lens through which millions interpreted scripture, history, and current events, especially those related to Israel. But to truly understand the scale of this influence, we must define who its adherents are and how their beliefs manifest in political and cultural life.

In the next chapter, we will explore who these Christian Zionists are, how their beliefs are defined, and why their sheer numbers have become one of the most powerful forces shaping American foreign policy toward Israel.

# Part IV
# The True Israel Lobby

# Chapter 9
## Who Is a Christian Zionist?

While most scholarly definitions of **Christian Zionism** emphasize its political activism, such as lobbying, fundraising, or direct engagement with foreign policy, I chose a broader and more behaviorally grounded definition. This book defines a **Christian Zionist** as anyone who believes that **Genesis 12:3 ("I will bless those who bless Israel...") refers to the modern state of Israel**. This belief, even when held passively, has profound political consequences. Dispensationalists who consider themselves "observers" rather than "agents" still shape U.S. foreign policy through their voting behavior, media consumption, and cultural influence. Their theological worldview informs how they vote, which candidates they support, and what policies they endorse, especially regarding Israel and Palestine (Blaising & Bock, 1993; Weber, 2004).

Moreover, this belief system drives market dynamics in American media. Christian Zionist audiences shaped by dispensationalist theology demand pro-Israel coverage and reject narratives that challenge Israeli actions. This creates a feedback loop where media outlets cater to theological bias, reinforcing public opinion and political inertia (Chomsky & Herman, 1988; Mangum & Sweetnam, 2009).

Therefore, limiting the definition of Christian Zionism to overt political activism misses the broader cultural and electoral impact of dispensationalist belief. The belief in Genesis 12:3 as a literal endorsement of modern Israel is not just theological, it is behavioral. It influences how people vote, how they interpret news, and how they respond to global events. This is why I define Christian Zionism not by activism, but by belief.

This definition allows us to move beyond denominational boundaries and theological nuances. It focuses on a single, measurable belief, one that has been consistently tracked in public opinion polls for decades.

## Measuring Belief: The Polling Data

Between **2000 and 2010**, multiple **Pew Research Center surveys** found that **between 40% and 45% of Americans** agreed with the statement that the biblical promise "*God will bless those who bless Israel*" applies to the modern state of Israel (Pew Research Center, 2003; 2005). This belief was especially strong among white evangelical Protestants, where support often exceeded 60%.

If we apply this definition to the U.S. population, the numbers are staggering. With a population of approximately 330 million, this means that **between 132 and 148 million Americans** qualify as Christian Zionists under this definition.

This is not a fringe group. It is a massive, mainstream segment of American society, larger than the entire population of Russia or Japan. It includes:

- **Evangelicals**, who emphasize personal conversion and biblical authority.
- **Pentecostals**, who stress the gifts of the Holy Spirit and end-times prophecy.

- **Charismatics**, who share Pentecostal beliefs but remain within mainline denominations like Catholicism, Anglicanism, or Lutheranism. Charismatics emphasize spiritual gifts such as speaking in tongues, healing, and prophecy, and are often deeply engaged with eschatological themes.
- Conservative Catholics and Messianic Jews.
- Viewers of prophecy-focused media like TBN, Daystar, and CBN.
- Churchgoers who have never heard the term "Christian Zionism" but believe in the divine significance of Israel.

## CUFI and the Power of Mobilization

One of the most prominent organizations representing Christian Zionists is **Christians United for Israel (CUFI)**, originally established in 1975 by Dr. David A. Lewis, but it was formally incorporated (registered) **by Pastor John Hagee in 2006**. CUFI describes itself as the **largest pro-Israel organization in the United States**. According to Hagee, CUFI has **over 10 million members** (CUFI, 2023).

While this number is impressive, it represents only a fraction of the broader Christian Zionist population. CUFI's membership is active, organized, and politically engaged, but the belief system it represents is far more widespread.

The difference between CUFI's membership and the broader Christian Zionist base is similar to the difference between registered voters and eligible voters. CUFI mobilizes. The rest believe. And when politicians pledge support for Israel, they are not just courting CUFI, they are signaling alignment with tens of millions of voters who see Israel as sacred.

*John Hagee (b. 1940)*

One of the most disturbing moments in the history of Christian Zionist rhetoric came when a prominent American preacher, John Hagee, suggested that Adolf Hitler was "a hunter" sent by God to drive Jews back to Israel. The comment, made in a sermon and later publicized during the 2008 U.S. presidential campaign, sparked outrage across religious and political communities. Hagee later apologized, but the statement revealed a deeper theological flaw: the tendency to interpret historical atrocities as divine instruments for prophecy fulfillment. This kind of thinking not only distorts history, it dehumanizes its victims and sanctifies their suffering (Spector, 2009).

## Jerry Falwell and the Moral Majority

The rise of Christian Zionism as a political force in the United States cannot be understood without examining the role of **Rev. Jerry Falwell** and the **Moral Majority**. Founded in 1979, the Moral Majority was a political organization that sought to mobilize conservative Christians around issues such as abortion, school prayer, and support for Israel.

Falwell preached that *"the Bible gives Israel title to all the land"*, and he frequently cited **Genesis 12:3** to argue that nations are blessed or cursed based on their stance toward Israel. In a 1983 interview, he declared: "God deals with nations in relation to how nations deal with Israel... I believe God has blessed America because we have blessed the Jews. If America turned against Israel, our value to God would cease" (Spector, 2009).

*Jerry Falwell (1933-2007)*

Falwell's influence extended beyond rhetoric. He developed a close relationship with Israeli Prime Minister **Menachem Begin**, received the **Jabotinsky Award**, and was gifted an Israeli-made **IAI 1124 Westwind** aircraft. He also opposed any land-for-peace compromise, asserting that the **West Bank should never be given back**. Begin reportedly shared Falwell's biblical perspective, believing Israel's borders would one day extend "from the Nile to the Euphrates."

Falwell's framing of support for Israel as a **moral imperative**, as if it were the only "moral" position for Christians, helped cement Christian Zionism as a central tenet of the Religious Right.

## Pat Robertson and the Televangelist Era

Another key figure in the rise of Christian Zionism was **Pat Robertson**, founder of the Christian Broadcasting Network (CBN) and host of *The 700 Club*. Robertson was one of the earliest televangelists to blend prophecy, politics, and media into a potent force for Christian Zionism.

Robertson echoed many of Falwell's views, frequently warning of **divine judgment** against nations that opposed Israel. He taught that the return of Jews to Israel was a fulfillment of prophecy and a prerequisite for the Second Coming of Christ. His broadcasts reached millions of viewers and helped normalize Christian Zionist theology in American households.

Robertson also used his platform to oppose peace initiatives like the **Oslo Accords**, arguing that any division of Jerusalem or Israeli withdrawal from occupied territories was contrary to God's will. His influence extended into politics, especially during the Reagan and Bush administrations, where he helped shape Christian Zionist support for pro-Israel policies.

*Pat Robertson (1930-2023)*

Together, Falwell and Robertson laid the groundwork for a generation of Christian Zionist leaders, including **John Hagee**, whose CUFI organization would later become the most visible face of the movement.

## Why This Matters

Understanding the **scale of Christian Zionism** is essential to understanding **American foreign policy**. While Jewish lobbying groups like the American Israel Public Affairs Committee (AIPAC) are often credited with shaping U.S. support for Israel, they represent a much smaller demographic. Jewish Americans make up about 2% of the U.S. population. Christian Zionists, by contrast, may represent **up to 45%**.

This theological base creates a political firewall around Israel. It ensures that support for Israel remains bipartisan, resilient, and often unquestioned. It also complicates efforts to advocate for Palestinian rights or a balanced approach to Middle East diplomacy.

Christian Zionists do not support Israel because of heritage or identity. They support it because they believe it is God's will. And that belief, reinforced in churches, Bible studies, and media, has become one of the most powerful forces in American politics.

## The Diversity Within Christian Zionism

It is important to note that **not all American Christians or evangelicals uniformly support every Israeli policy**. That would be an over gener-alization. While a strong majority do, there is diversity. Certain evangelical voices, such as Tony Campolo, or denominations like the Mennonites, have criticized Israel's occupation and called for justice and peace (Spector, 2009).

Moreover, mainline Protestant denominations, the Catholic Church, and Eastern Orthodox Christians generally do not endorse dispensationalist prophecy doctrines. Many Christians interpret Bible prophecies in non-literal or non-political ways. For example, the Middle East Council of Churches and numerous theologians have outright criticized Christian Zionism as a distortion of Christian teaching (Ariel, 2013).

## The Endgame Paradox

Christian Zionists believe Jews must return to Israel and rebuild a temple to fulfill prophecy. But classical dispensational prophecy also holds that eventually many Jews will either convert to Christianity or face great tribulation. Critics point out a moral irony: the support is not entirely altruistic, as it envisions a scenario where Jews play a role in Christian eschatology, potentially leading to mass death in Armageddon.

Some Israelis question whether such "support" is truly pro-Jewish. It's worth highlighting this paradox as a flaw in Christian Zionist logic, they profess love for Jews and Israel, yet their theology ultimately expects Jews to accept Jesus or suffer in the end times (Sizer, 2004).

## A Personal Reflection

During my conversations with Americans, many times when I mentioned that Palestinians are not only Muslims but also proud of our substantial Christian community, one that traces its roots to the earliest Christians in the world, the response was often a puzzled look. They would either say something like, "But are they truly *Christian*?" or there would be silence.

I never understood that silence at the time. But now, I understand it as the switch in the mind that got turned on, along with a voice in their head saying, "These are the non-believing Christians who will not be raptured."

This theological reflex is not just anti-Palestinian, it is anti-human.

Palestinian Christians, the indigenous Arab followers of Christ whose roots trace back to the earliest Church, are themselves victims of the same ethnic cleansing campaign waged against the Palestinian people. The first Christian communities, the oldest churches on earth, and their clergy are being systematically forced out of the Holy Land. Churches are desecrated, cemeteries vandalized, and clergy harassed by settler-colonial zealots, while Christian Zionists turn a blind eye. This is not only an assault on a people but on the very cradle of Christianity.

Preserving the Christian presence in Palestine is not a matter of diversity, it is a matter of justice and historical continuity. As the Kairos Palestine document affirms: *"The hemorrhage of Christian emigration has not stopped, and this emigration poses a real threat to the Christian presence in Palestine, which is now threatened with ethnic cleansing and extinction"* (Kairos Palestine, 2025, §1-17). Church leaders in Jerusalem have warned that these policies are part of a systematic effort to empty the Holy Land of Christians (§1-8). This reality demands urgent global Christian solidarity, not silence or complicity.

Now that we've defined who Christian Zionists are and quantified their presence, we turn to the cultural machinery that sustains their worldview. In the next chapter, we will explore how dispensationalist theology permeates American pop culture and politics, from bestselling novels to media bias, from church pulpits to congressional offices. We will see how the Rapture became a cultural symbol, and how Christian Zionism evolved into a powerful political force that shapes not only beliefs, but behavior.

# Chapter 10
## Pop Culture, Politics, and the Rapture

Chapter 7

Top Talent, Politics, and the Future

In the previous chapter, we established that between 132 and 148 million Americans, roughly 40–45% of the population, believe that the biblical phrase "God will bless those who bless Israel" refers to the modern state of Israel. This belief defines them as Christian Zionists. With such staggering numbers, it becomes clear that Christian Zionism is not a fringe movement, it is a cultural force. And like all cultural forces, it expresses itself through media, politics, and public imagination.

## Influence on Media and Literature

Dispensationalist theology, with its vivid imagery of the Rapture, the Antichrist, and the battle of Armageddon, has long captivated American audiences. Its themes have permeated books, films, music, and television, transforming theological speculation into cultural narrative.

The most iconic example is the **Left Behind** series by **Tim LaHaye** and **Jerry B. Jenkins**, which sold **over 80 million copies worldwide** (LaHaye & Jenkins, 1995–2007). These novels dramatize the Rapture and its aftermath, portraying a world plunged into chaos as believers vanish and the Antichrist rises to power. The success of *Left Behind* was not accidental, it tapped into a theological framework that tens of millions already believed. Scofield's annotations had primed generations of readers to expect a literal fulfillment of Revelation, and the series offered a gripping narrative that aligned perfectly with those expectations (Mangum & Sweetnam, 2009).

Other pop culture references include:

- *The Omega Code* (1999), a film dramatizing biblical prophecy and the rise of the Antichrist.
- *Thief in the Night* (1972), a Christian film that became a cult classic among evangelicals.
- Rapture-themed music, such as Larry Norman's "I Wish We'd All Been Ready," which became an anthem for evangelical youth.
- Prophecy-focused programming on networks like TBN and Daystar, which interpret current events through a dispensationalist lens (Weber, 2004).

These cultural products do more than entertain, they reinforce a worldview. They tell millions of Americans that history is unfolding according to a divine script, and that they are living in the final chapters.

## Political Implications and Cultural Symbols

The cultural saturation of **dispensationalism** has profound political consequences. For many, prophecy-themed media reinforced political choices as spiritual obligations. **Christian Zionist voters**, shaped by **Scofield's theology** and its cultural echoes, prioritize candidates who align with their **eschatological views**. Support for Israel becomes a litmus test for political legitimacy. Politicians who pledge unwavering support for the Jewish state are seen not just as allies, but as instruments of prophecy (Spector, 2009).

## Harry Truman: The Biblical President

President **Harry S. Truman** recognized the State of Israel just **11 minutes** after its declaration of independence in 1948. While strategic and humanitarian factors played a role, Truman's decision was also deeply personal. He grew up reading the Bible and reportedly likened himself to **King Cyrus**, the Persian ruler who enabled Jews to return to Jerusalem. In 1953, Truman met Jewish leaders and declared, "I am Cyrus" (Ariel, 2013). This biblical self-identification set a precedent for future presidents who viewed support for Israel as a spiritual duty.

*Harry S. Truman (1884-1972)*

## The Rise of the Religious Right and Reagan

The 1967 Six-Day War electrified American Christian Zionists, who saw Israel's victory as a miraculous fulfillment of prophecy. This catalyzed the rise of organized Christian Zionism in the late 1970s and 1980s.

In 1981, when the Reagan administration considered selling AWACS surveillance planes to Saudi Arabia, **Rev. Jerry Falwell's** Moral Majority joined Israeli officials in opposing the sale. Though the sale went through, the episode demonstrated how Christian Zionists could act as a lobbying force aligned with Israeli interests.

President **Ronald Reagan** was sympathetic to evangelical views. In 1982, he told the Israeli lobby, "I turn back to the pages of the Bible, to the prophets of the Old Testament and the signs foretelling Armageddon, and I find myself wondering if... we're the generation that is going to see that come about" (Weber, 2004).

*Ronald Reagan (1911-2004)*

## George W. Bush and the Evangelical Base

Under **President George W. Bush (2001–2009)**, Christian evangelicals were a core constituency. Bush endorsed an Israeli plan to retain major West Bank settlements in 2004, pleasing Christian Zionists. However, he also pursued the "Roadmap for Peace," which included a vision of a Palestinian state, highlighting the tension between evangelical influence and broader strategic interests.

*George W. Bush (b. 1946)*

## Donald Trump and the Prophetic Presidency

President **Donald Trump (2017–2021)** enacted policies celebrated by Christian Zionists:

- Moved the U.S. Embassy to **Jerusalem** in 2018.
- Recognized Israeli sovereignty over the **Golan Heights** in 2019.
- Cut aid to Palestinians and withdrew from international agreements seen as unfavorable to Israel.

Trump's evangelical advisory council included vocal Christian Zionists like Mike Pence and Mike Pompeo. When the Jerusalem embassy opened, Pastor John Hagee spoke at the ceremony, underscoring the movement's influence.

Polls showed over 80% of white evangelical Christians approved of Trump, many citing his stance on Israel. While strategic and political factors also played a role, Christian Zionist enthusiasm was undeniably a major influence.

*Donald Trump (b. 1946)*

This influence has been visible across administrations. In 2011, when the Obama administration considered abstaining from a United Nations Security Council resolution condemning Israeli settlements, Christian Zionist groups strongly objected, framing the move as a betrayal of biblical promises to Israel (Spector, 2009). Their pressure contributed to the U.S. ultimately vetoing the resolution, despite broad international support for it.

In 2020, when the Trump administration unveiled its "Peace to Prosperity" plan, which allowed for the annexation of large parts of the West Bank, Christian Zionist leaders praised the proposal as a prophetic milestone. Organizations like Christians United for Israel (CUFI) celebrated the plan's alignment with biblical boundaries, while Palestinians and international observers condemned it as a blueprint for apartheid and permanent occupation (CUFI, 2020; ReliefWeb, 2025).

This theological-political fusion continues to manifest in real time, not only in policy decisions but in the rhetoric of high-profile political figures. A recent exchange between two prominent conservatives, Tucker Carlson and Senator Ted Cruz, offers a striking example of how deeply embedded Christian Zionist theology remains in American political discourse.

# Tucker Carlson vs. Ted Cruz: A Modern Flashpoint

*Ted Cruz (b. 1970)*

*Tucker Carlson (b. 1969)*

In a widely circulated interview aired on **June 18, 2025**, conservative commentator **Tucker Carlson** challenged **Senator Ted Cruz** on his unwavering support for Israel amid the ongoing war in Gaza. Carlson, known for his nationalist and often contrarian views, questioned why American politicians continue to prioritize Israel's interests even when its actions, particularly in Gaza, have drawn international condemnation for human rights violations.

In response, Senator Cruz invoked a familiar refrain among Christian Zionists: "The Bible says, 'I will bless those who bless Israel and curse those who curse Israel.' That's not just a suggestion, it's a promise from God". Cruz's statement echoed the foundational belief of Christian Zionism: that unwavering support for the modern state of Israel is not merely a political stance, but a spiritual imperative.

Carlson pushed back, asking whether such a view should override American interests or moral accountability. He questioned whether it was appropriate to base foreign policy on a literal interpretation of ancient scripture, especially when it leads to the justification of civilian casualties and the erosion of international law.

This exchange was more than a political disagreement, it was a theological confrontation. Carlson's challenge exposed the tension between nationalist conservatism and Christian Zionist eschatology. It also revealed how deeply Genesis 12:3 continues to function as a litmus test for political orthodoxy among American Christian Zionists and their elected representatives.

The moment was significant not only for its content but for its symbolism. It marked a rare instance in which a major conservative figure publicly questioned the theological assumptions that have long underpinned bipartisan support for Israel. It also signaled a potential shift in the discourse, one where even within conservative circles, the automatic invocation of prophecy as policy is no longer immune to scrutiny.

This exchange between Carlson and Cruz underscores the enduring power of Christian Zionist theology in shaping political discourse. It also reveals cracks in the once-unified front of conservative support for Israel, cracks that may widen as more voices begin to question the moral and theological foundations of this alliance.

These episodes illustrate how Christian Zionist theology continues to shape U.S. policy, not only through electoral influence but also through direct lobbying and public pressure. The result is a foreign policy that often prioritizes prophecy over peace.

This theological-political fusion manifests in symbolic ways. Bumper stickers reading "In case of Rapture, this car will be unmanned" became common in evangelical communities. Congressional offices displayed signs that read, "In case of Rapture, this office will be empty." These slogans are not jokes, they are declarations of belief, signaling that the Rapture is imminent and that political engagement is part of a divine mission (Weber, 2004). Among those who have displayed such signs are former Congressman Randy Forbes and Representative Michele Bachmann, both of whom have publicly aligned with Christian Zionist beliefs.

It is important to note that most of the American public, especially devout Christians, are good and well-intentioned individuals. They would not normally accept the suffering of other human beings. However, when it comes to the issue of Israel, it becomes a deeply religious and personal matter. The belief that Israel is central to God's plan overrides moral discomfort. The suffering of Palestinians is not ignored out of cruelty, but out of theological necessity.

Most Christian Zionists are not aware that they hold this distinction from other Christians around the world. They are unaware of the history of dispensationalism, and the vast majority do not realize that their beliefs, if taken to their theological conclusion, ultimately lead to the demise of all Jews and most of humanity. They are not malicious. They are misinformed.

## The Gaza Genocide and the Theology of Silence

To understand how theology can shape real-world violence, we must examine how Christian Zionist beliefs have influenced responses to recent events in Gaza.

Since October 2023, the world has witnessed a genocide in Gaza. Entire neighborhoods have been reduced to rubble. Hospitals, schools, and refugee camps, Mosques, and even some of the oldest churches in the world, have been bombed. Tens of thousands of civilians, many of them children, have been killed or maimed. The suffering is visible to anyone willing to look. And yet, among many Christian Zionist communities in the United States, there is silence. Or worse, celebration.

This silence is not accidental. It is theological.

Christian Zionism, rooted in dispensationalist theology, teaches that Israel's actions, no matter how violent, are part of a divine script. The suffering of Palestinians is not seen as a humanitarian crisis, but as a prophetic necessity. To question Israel's conduct is to question God's plan. To empathize with Gaza is to betray scripture.

In 2024, this theology has manifested in overt political and financial support for Israel's military campaign in Gaza. Organizations like Christians United for Israel (CUFI) continue to raise millions of dollars for Israeli causes, including military and settlement infrastructure. This fundraising persists even as international bodies accuse Israel of war crimes and deliberate starvation tactics (CUFI, 2024; ReliefWeb, 2025). These donations are not framed as humanitarian aid, they are framed as prophecy fulfillment.

The theological firewall around Israeli violence has hardened. In churches, media outlets, and evangelical conferences, the destruction of Gaza is interpreted as a necessary step toward the Second Coming. Empathy for Palestinians is discouraged, even condemned. The suffering of civilians is not ignored out of cruelty, it is ignored out of theological obligation.

In April 2024, reports emerged that CUFI and affiliated ministries had increased fundraising efforts in response to the war, framing their campaigns as "standing with Israel in its prophetic hour". These efforts were accompanied by sermons and broadcasts that described the war as a "divine cleansing" and a "necessary confrontation with evil." Such language sanctifies violence and erases the humanity of its victims.

Meanwhile, the Israeli military has bombed designated safe zones, refugee tents, and UN shelters in Gaza, violating international humanitarian law (ReliefWeb, 2025). Yet Christian Zionist leaders have remained silent, or have justified these actions as part of God's plan. The theology does not merely tolerate genocide, it rationalizes it.

This is the ultimate consequence of dispensationalist theology. It is not just antisemitic. It is anti-human.

And it is no longer fringe. It is mainstream. It shapes U.S. foreign policy, influences elections, and mobilizes millions. It has turned empathy into heresy and genocide into gospel.

To confront Christian Zionism is not just to challenge a theology. It is to reclaim our shared humanity.

## Financial Support from Christian Organizations

Beyond political influence, American Christian organizations provide substantial financial support to Israel. Evangelical churches and ministries raise millions of dollars annually for Israeli causes, often framed as fulfilling biblical prophecy. These funds support:

- Settlement expansion in the West Bank - Illegal under International Law.
- Humanitarian aid for Jewish immigrants (aliyah) returning to Israel.
- Security infrastructure, including bomb shelters and surveillance systems.
- Temple-related projects, such as the Temple Institute in Jerusalem, which prepares for the rebuilding of Solomon's Temple.

Estimates vary, but some reports suggest that evangelical donations to Israel exceed **$100 million annually**. One of the most influential conduits for this funding is the **International Fellowship of Christians and Jews (IFCJ)**, which since the 1990s has channeled hundreds of millions of dollars from evangelical donors to Israel. These funds have supported a wide range of initiatives, including social welfare programs, security infrastructure, and immigration assistance for Jews making aliyah (Spector, 2009; IFCJ, 2024). Alongside organizations like **Christians United for Israel (CUFI)**, IFCJ has helped institutionalize a theology of financial support, where giving to Israel is framed not as charity, but as prophecy fulfillment.

This private financial support complements the **$3.8 billion in annual military aid** that the U.S. government provides to Israel. While government aid is strategic and diplomatic, evangelical donations are theological. They are not about defense, they are about destiny.

In the next chapter, we will explore one of the most urgent and controversial goals of Christian Zionism: the push to rebuild Solomon's Temple in Jerusalem. We will examine its theological roots, political implications, and the dangerous consequences of turning prophecy into policy.

# Part V
# The Temple and the Apocalypse

# Chapter 11
## The Push to Rebuild Solomon's Temple

## Historical and Theological Context of the Temple

**Solomon's Temple**, built in the **10th century BCE**, was the centerpiece of ancient Jewish worship. Commissioned by **King Solomon**, it was designed to house the **Ark of the Covenant** and serve as the dwelling place of God on Earth. The Temple's most sacred space, the Holy of Holies, was believed to contain the divine presence itself. Worship was centralized in this structure, Jews were required to make pilgrimages to Jerusalem, and sacrifices could only be performed at the Temple (Spector, 2009).

Until its destruction by the **Babylonians in 586 BCE**, the Temple was the exclusive site of Jewish religious life. Its loss during the Babylonian captivity triggered a theological crisis: how could one worship God without access to His house?

During this exile, Jewish theology underwent a profound transformation. Scholars and prophets began to teach that God's presence was not confined to a building. Instead, the divine could dwell within individuals. This shift gave rise to the concept that the body is a temple and that worship could occur anywhere. It laid the foundation for rabbinic Judaism and the synagogue system, which decentralized worship and emphasized study, prayer, and ethical living (Ariel, 2013).

Today, most **Jewish denominations** do not prioritize rebuilding the Temple. It is viewed as **symbolic, not essential**. But for **Christian Zionists**, the Temple is **critical**. According to dispensationalist theology, the rebuilding of Solomon's Temple is a prerequisite for the fulfillment of end-times prophecy. It is believed that the Antichrist will enter the rebuilt Temple, declare himself divine, and trigger the final battle of Armageddon (Mangum & Sweetnam, 2009).

This belief is not rooted in Jewish theology, it is a Christian eschatological construct. The Temple must be rebuilt so that prophecy can be fulfilled, the Antichrist can rise, and Jesus can return. For Christian Zionists, the Temple is not a relic, it is a countdown clock.

## Christian Zionist Motivations for Rebuilding

Christian Zionists support the Temple's reconstruction not out of reverence for Jewish tradition. They support it because it fits into their prophetic timeline. Ministries, churches, and media outlets promote the idea that the Temple's reconstruction is imminent. Organizations like the Temple Institute in Jerusalem receive financial support from American evangelicals who see their donations as part of a divine mission (Spector, 2009).

The irony is stark: Christian Zionists support a Jewish religious project that most Jews do not prioritize, and they do so with the expectation that it will ultimately lead to the destruction of Israel and the death of all non-believers. Yet most Christian Zionists are unaware of this theological endpoint. They believe they are supporting God's plan, not hastening global catastrophe.

## Appeasement Politics: Israeli Signals to Evangelical Backers

There is growing evidence that Israeli politicians and religious organizations emphasize the rebuilding of the Temple, and escalate tensions around Masjid Al Aqsa, not solely for domestic religious reasons, but to appease their Christian Zionist backers in the United States. The Temple Mount is one of the most sensitive religious sites in the world, and any provocation there has global consequences.

Yet Israeli politicians, including members of the Knesset and far-right parties, have repeatedly called for increased Jewish access to the Temple Mount and have supported organizations that advocate for rebuilding the Temple. These actions often coincide with fundraising campaigns and political outreach to evangelical communities in the U.S., who see such moves as prophetic milestones (Weber, 2004).

The increased assaults and provocations around Masjid Al Aqsa, such as unauthorized visits by Israeli officials, calls to change the status quo, and support for Temple-focused NGOs, are often framed as religious freedom issues. But they also serve as symbolic gestures to American evangelicals, signaling that Israel is fulfilling its divine role.

This strategy is not hidden. Israeli leaders frequently speak at Christian Zionist conferences, including CUFI's annual summit, where they emphasize Jerusalem's centrality and the Temple's prophetic significance. These speeches are tailored to resonate with dispensationalist theology, reinforcing the alliance between Israeli nationalism and American evangelical eschatology (Spector, 2009).

## Jerusalem as Capital and the Antichrist Prophecy

**Jerusalem** holds a central place in **Christian Zionist eschatology**. It is believed that during the **millennial Kingdom**, Christ will rule from Jerusalem, seated in the rebuilt Temple. This belief has led many evangelicals to support policies that increase Israeli control over the Temple Mount, even at the expense of Palestinian rights and regional stability (Weber, 2004).

In the 1967 six-day war, Israel occupied the West Bank which included the eastern part of Jerusalem. Then almost immediately extended its law, jurisdiction, and administration to East Jerusalem and surrounding areas. This move was widely interpreted as annexation. Annexation of territory acquired through military force is considered illegal under international law and violates the foundational principles of the United Nations Charter. In 1980, Israel passed the *Jerusalem Law*, declaring "complete and united Jerusalem" as the capital of Israel, formalizing the annexation under Israeli law. The United Nations and most countries around the world have refused to recognize it as Israel's capital, citing its contested status and the need for a negotiated settlement. The U.S. Congress passed the Jerusalem Embassy Act in 1995, calling for the embassy to be moved, but every president until Donald Trump signed waivers delaying the move.

In 2017, President Trump broke with precedent and officially recognized Jerusalem as Israel's capital, moving the U.S. embassy there in 2018. This decision was widely celebrated by Christian Zionists as a prophetic milestone. It was seen as a divine endorsement of Israel's sovereignty over Jerusalem and a step closer to the fulfillment of end-times prophecy.

But for Palestinians, the move was devastating. It signaled the abandonment of U.S. neutrality and the erosion of hopes for a two-state solution. It sided with the Israeli annexation of East Jerusalem, illegal under international law, which Palestinians see as the capital of their future state. The embassy move was not just symbolic, it was a geopolitical earthquake.

This theological-political fusion is not confined to sermons or symbolic gestures, it manifests in real-time diplomacy. One of the clearest examples came in September 2024, when Israeli Prime Minister Benjamin Netanyahu addressed the United Nations.

## Netanyahu's UN Maps: A Dog Whistle to Christian Zionists

### "The Blessing" and "The Curse": Netanyahu's Prophetic Signal to Christian Zionists

On September 27, 2024, Israeli Prime Minister Benjamin Netanyahu stood before the United Nations General Assembly and held up two maps of the Middle East. One was labeled "The Blessing," the other "The Curse." To most observers, this was a theatrical flourish, perhaps a geopolitical metaphor. But to Christian Zionists, it was a thunderous dog whistle.

Netanyahu's use of these two words was not random. It was a deliberate invocation of Genesis 12:3, the foundational verse of Christian Zionist theology:

> *"I will bless those who bless you, and whoever curses you I will curse."* (Genesis 12:3, NIV)

This verse is interpreted by Christian Zionists as a divine command to support the modern state of Israel. It is repeated in sermons, printed on bumper stickers, and embedded in the Scofield Reference Bible's annotations (Mangum & Sweetnam, 2009). For millions of Christian Zionists, this verse is not symbolic, it is literal, and it governs their political choices, foreign policy views, and moral compass.

By labeling one map "The Blessing" and the other "The Curse," Netanyahu was not speaking to the diplomats in the room. He was speaking to the Christian Zionist base, particularly in the United States. He was signaling that nations who support Israel will be divinely rewarded, and those who oppose it will be punished. This binary framing is central to dispensationalist theology, which divides history into cycles of obedience and judgment.

But there is a deeper layer to this moment, one that reveals the strategic cynicism of Jewish Zionist leadership.

Jewish Zionist leaders, including Netanyahu, fully understand the Christian Zionist worldview. They know that Christian Zionism is not truly pro-Jewish. They know that its endgame is either the conversion or annihilation of Jews in the final battle of Armageddon (Spector, 2009; Weber, 2004). They know that Christian Zionists support Israel not out of solidarity, but out of eschatological necessity.

And yet, they embrace this support.

Why? Because it is politically useful. Financially powerful. Militarily strategic. Diplomatically essential.

Netanyahu's map stunt was not a theological endorsement, it was a transactional signal. It said to Christian Zionists: "We know what you believe. We don't share your endgame. But we'll play along, because your support serves our interests."

This is the paradox at the heart of the Christian–Jewish Zionist alliance. One side believes it is fulfilling prophecy. The other side is using that belief to advance its own nationalist agenda. One side anticipates the destruction of the Jews. The other side is willing to tolerate that theology, as long as it delivers weapons, votes, and diplomatic cover.

This alliance is not built on shared values. It is built on mutual exploitation.

Netanyahu's maps were not just symbolic, they were strategic. They activated the theological reflexes of Christian Zionists, reminding them that support for Israel is not just political, it is spiritual. And in doing so, he reinforced the alliance that has turned prophecy into policy and theology into war.

For most Palestinians, Netanyahu's UN stunt was confusing, even surreal. The gesture, holding up maps labeled "The Blessing" and "The Curse", seemed theatrical, perhaps symbolic, but its deeper theological significance was not immediately understood. Few realized that this was not just a political flourish, but a direct invocation of Genesis 12:3, the foundational verse of Christian Zionist theology. In that moment, our suffering was not merely ignored, it was reframed as a prophetic necessity.

Our humanity was not just erased, it was replaced with scripture. What we saw as genocide, Christian Zionists interpreted as gospel. This moment marked a turning point, not in diplomacy, but in theology. It reminded us that the battle we face is not only against occupation, but against a belief system that sanctifies it.

Netanyahu's speech was not an isolated moment, it was part of a broader strategy that leverages Christian Zionist theology to entrench Israeli policy. This dynamic has profound implications for U.S. diplomacy, especially regarding the two-state solution.

## U.S. Reluctance Toward the Two-State Solution

The two-state solution has long been recognized as the most viable path to peace between Israelis and Palestinians. It is supported by the United Nations.

the European Union, and most international actors. It promises security for Israel, a form of statehood for Palestinians, and a framework for coexistence.

Yet the U.S. has been reluctant to push Israel toward this solution. While successive administrations have paid lip service to the idea, meaningful pressure has been absent. Settlements continue to expand, negotiations stall, and the status quo persists.

This reluctance is not just political, it is theological. For Christian Zionists, the idea of Israel giving up land it occupied militarily in 1967 in exchange for peace with all the Arab nations, contradicts prophecy. The land was given by God, and to surrender it is to defy divine will. Politicians who rely on Christian Zionist support are acutely aware of this. They know that advocating for a two-state solution could alienate millions of voters who see territorial compromise as spiritual betrayal.

This theological resistance has real-world consequences. It prevents diplomatic progress, entrenches occupation, and perpetuates suffering. It turns prophecy into policy and belief into blockade.

The obsession with rebuilding the Temple is not an isolated theological aspiration, it is embedded within a broader ecosystem of influence that shapes American foreign policy and domestic politics. To understand why this vision commands such unwavering support, we must examine the structural forces that translate prophecy into policy. These forces do not operate in a vacuum; they form a triangle of power, media bias, lobbying leverage, and a vast Christian Zionist electorate, that hijacks democratic processes and reorients national priorities toward Israel. This triangle is not merely a political phenomenon; it is a theological engine disguised as democracy. The next chapter unpacks this dynamic in detail, revealing how belief, money, and messaging converge to transform America's political landscape into '**Israel First**.'

# Chapter 12
## The Triangle of Influence:
## How Media, Money, and
## Theology Hijack American Democracy

In a **democracy**, politicians compete for votes and require substantial funding to reach as many voters as possible. When **40–45% of the electorate** holds a deeply seated conviction about **Israel**, candidates naturally lean toward that point of view to attract as many voters as possible. This dynamic is amplified by the fact that the remaining 55–60% of the population does not hold strong views on Israel. The result is a powerful mechanism that biases the entire political system, at local, state, and federal levels, toward unwavering support for Israel. Yet this electoral reality does not operate in isolation. It intersects with two other forces, media bias and lobbying power, forming a triangle that reshapes U.S. politics into **"Israel First" rather than "America First."**

## Arm One: The Christian Zionist Electorate

For **Christian Zionist voters**, support for **Israel** is not merely a foreign policy preference, **it is a spiritual imperative**. Dispensationalist theology, popularized by the Scofield Reference Bible and reinforced through decades of sermons, media, and cultural products, teaches that Israel's survival and territorial integrity are prerequisites for the Second Coming of Christ (Mangum & Sweetnam, 2009). This belief transforms political allegiance into a matter of eternal consequence. Candidates who pledge unconditional support for Israel are perceived not just as allies, but as instruments of prophecy. Conversely, those who advocate for Palestinian rights or territorial compromise risk being cast as opponents of God's plan.

The electoral implications are profound. In competitive districts, especially across the Bible Belt and Midwest, Christian Zionist voters can tip the balance in primaries and general elections. Their influence extends beyond voting behavior to campaign financing, grassroots mobilization, and media consumption. For politicians, aligning with Christian Zionist priorities is not optional, it is existential.

## Arm Two: The Israel Lobby and Financial Leverage

The second arm of the triangle is the **Israel lobby**, spearheaded by the **American Israel Public Affairs Committee (AIPAC)** and supported by allied organizations such as **Christians United for Israel (CUFI)**. While Jewish Americans constitute only about 2% of the U.S. population. Even if we assume that AIPAC represents the interests of all the American Jewry, which it does not, and even if we assume that all Jewish Americans have a vested interest in supporting Israel unconditionally, which they do not;  AIPAC still wields disproportionate influence through strategic campaign contributions, policy advocacy, and symbolic endorsements. Its annual conferences attract bipartisan participation, with candidates and incumbents competing to deliver speeches affirming their loyalty to Israel.

AIPAC's power operates on two levels. First, it provides substantial financial support to candidates who demonstrate unwavering commitment to Israel. This funding is not limited to congressional races; it permeates state legislatures, governorships, and even local offices. Second, AIPAC's public endorsements function as a theological signal to Christian Zionist voters. When a candidate appears at an AIPAC event or issues a statement of allegiance, it communicates more than political alignment, it conveys spiritual fidelity. For millions of Christian Zionists, such gestures confirm that the candidate is "on God's side."

This dual mechanism, financial leverage and symbolic resonance, creates a formidable incentive structure. Politicians who comply are rewarded with campaign funds and electoral support. Those who dissent face financial marginalization and theological vilification. The result is a policy environment where unconditional support for Israel becomes a prerequisite for political survival, regardless of its implications for U.S. interests or international law.

## Arm Three: Mainstream Media Bias and Audience Alignment

The third arm of the triangle is **media bias**, driven not solely by ownership patterns but by **audience demand**. Contrary to simplistic narratives that attribute pro-Israel coverage to Jewish control of mainstream media conglomerates, the reality is more complex. Market dynamics play a decisive role. Media outlets cater to their readership, and when that readership includes tens of millions of Christian Zionists, editorial choices reflect theological preferences.

Consider the predicament of a newspaper publisher. If the paper reports honestly on Israel's actions, highlighting the occupation, the displacement of Palestinians, or the destruction of homes, it risks alienating Christian Zionist subscribers. These readers do not seek balanced coverage; they seek affirmation of their worldview. Failure to provide that affirmation results in canceled subscriptions, declining ratings, and financial loss. Consequently, media corporations adopt a narrative that aligns with dispensationalist theology, portraying Israel as heroic and Palestinians as obstacles to peace.

This bias is reinforced by the ideological orientation of journalists themselves. Many reporters within conservative media ecosystems share Christian Zionist convictions, viewing their work as a form of ministry rather than mere reportage. Even those who do not share these beliefs face institutional pressures to conform. Career advancement often depends on editorial compliance, creating a culture where dissenting voices are silenced and critical perspectives are marginalized.

The outcome is a feedback loop: theological demand shapes media content, media content reinforces theological conviction, and both converge to sustain political inertia. As Chomsky and Herman (1988) argue in *Manufacturing Consent*, media systems often serve elite interests. In the case of Israel, they also serve eschatological ones.

## The Self-Perpetuating Loop

When these three forces, **electoral theology, lobbying power, and media bias**, interact, they create a **self-perpetuating loop** that hijacks **American democracy**. Christian Zionist voters demand pro-Israel policies; media outlets validate those demands; lobbying organizations reward compliance with financial support. Each arm of the triangle amplifies the others, producing a political ecosystem where dissent is punished, empathy is silenced, and foreign allegiance masquerades as patriotism.

This dynamic is not merely theoretical, it manifests in concrete policy outcomes. The United States provides Israel with $3.8 billion in annual military aid, vetoes United Nations resolutions condemning settlement expansion, and recognizes territorial annexations that violate international law (ReliefWeb, 2025). These actions are justified not through strategic calculus, but through theological rhetoric. Politicians invoke Genesis 12:3 as readily as they cite national security, framing foreign policy as an act of obedience to God rather than a function of democratic deliberation.

The consequences are catastrophic. By subordinating national interest to prophetic expectation, the triangle erodes the foundations of representative government. It transforms foreign policy into a sacrament, where scripture overrides statute and eschatology eclipses ethics. It redirects billions of dollars from domestic priorities, healthcare, education, infrastructure, toward a foreign state whose actions often contravene international norms. And it perpetuates a cycle of violence in the Middle East, where peace initiatives are sabotaged by theological absolutism.

## Hijacking Democracy: From America First to Israel First

The triangle of influence does more than distort policy, it redefines patriotism. In this inverted moral economy, loyalty to Israel becomes a litmus test for loyalty to God, and by extension, loyalty to America. Candidates who question this alignment are branded as heretics, traitors, or worse. Media outlets amplify these accusations, while lobbying organizations enforce them through financial sanctions. The result is a political culture where theological orthodoxy supplants constitutional principles, and prophetic fidelity eclipses democratic accountability.

This is not democracy, it is theocratic capture of statecraft. It is a system where the will of the majority is subordinated to the eschatological fantasies of a minority, and where public policy is scripted not in congressional chambers but in pulpits and prophecy conferences. It is a system that sanctifies suffering, erases empathy, and weaponizes faith against justice.

## Conclusion: Breaking the Triangle

To restore democratic integrity, the triangle must be dismantled. This requires confronting each of its Arms: educating voters about the manmade origins of dispensationalist theology, exposing the financial mechanisms of lobbying organizations, and challenging the market-driven bias of media systems. It demands a reorientation of political discourse, from prophecy to policy, from eschatology to ethics, from Israel First to America First.

The stakes could not be higher. As long as the triangle remains intact, American democracy will continue to serve a foreign agenda at the expense of its own citizens. And the suffering of Palestinians will remain invisible, erased not by ignorance, but by theology masquerading as truth.

The triangle of influence explains how Christian Zionism institutionalizes its power, through votes, dollars, and headlines. But this machinery does more than shape policy; it shapes perception. It constructs a moral firewall that silences empathy and reframes injustice as divine necessity. To grasp the full impact of this ideology, we must move beyond its structural mechanics and confront its psychological reflex, the moment when compassion collapses under the weight of prophecy. This is the switch in the mind: a manufactured response that turns suffering into scripture and genocide into gospel. The following chapter explores this phenomenon, exposing how Christian Zionism not only distorts politics but dehumanizes entire populations in the name of faith.

# Chapter 13
## The Switch in the Mind
## Christian Zionism as
## Antisemitic and Anti-Human

To my fellow Palestinians, and to all who have stood with us in solidarity, there is a truth we must confront with clarity and courage.

For over a century, since the Balfour Declaration of 1917 and the British Mandate that followed, we have fought to reclaim our land, our dignity, and our right to exist. We have resisted occupation, endured ethnic cleansing, and survived the machinery of apartheid. We have buried our children, defended our homes, and clung to our heritage as it was stolen and repackaged as someone else's. We have fought with everything we had, stones, words, memory, and hope.

**But we have been fighting the shadow, not the ideological engine.**

For decades, we were led to believe that our enemy was **Jewish Zionism, the ideology that created the Israeli state and justified our dispossession.** We believed that the state of Israel was the root of our suffering: the occupation, the apartheid, the ethnic cleansing. And we fought it with everything we had. But now, we must confront a **deeper truth**. Behind the visible machinery of Zionism lies a theological engine that has fueled it for centuries. What we have been fighting all along was not the ideological engine itself, but its shadow.

The visible limbs, Jewish Zionism and the Israeli state, were animated by something older, larger, and more deeply embedded in the global order: Christian Zionism. It is Christian Zionism that gave birth to Jewish Zionism, that armed it, sanctified it, and globalized its reach. It is Christian Zionism that turned our dispossession into prophecy, our suffering into scripture, and our erasure into divine fulfillment.

This is not just a theology, it is a geopolitical engine, a colonial blueprint, and a spiritual justification for genocide. And unless we understand it, confront it, and dismantle it, the shadow will keep growing.

When I first arrived in the United States, one of the most common questions I was asked was, "Why do you hate the Jews?" My answer was always the same: "We don't. We have no reason to. For centuries, Jews lived among us in peace. Jewish communities were part of our culture, our cities, our history. This is not a religious war. We do not fight Israel because they are Jewish. We fight because we are occupied. Because our rights are denied. Because our homes are stolen."

Back then, I believed that the conflict with Israel was not a religious one, but merely a political one centred on human rights.

There are many factors that converged and conspired to shape our suffering, including geopolitical, colonial, economic, and political interests and ambitions. Not the least of which is the deeply-seated antisemitic sentiments in Europe that drove the desire to get the Jewish communities out of Europe. It is important to realize that there has always been a religious war waged against us, one we failed to see. The frontlines may be manned by Jewish Zionists, but the armies behind them are Christian Zionists. Certain theological interpretations have led some to view Palestinian suffering as part of a prophetic narrative, an outlook that can unintentionally justify injustice. They are the ones who see our suffering not as injustice, but as divine choreography.

This is not just about saving Palestine. This is about saving humanity from a theology that anticipates global upheaval in the name of redemption. A theology that believes the world must burn before it can be reborn. A theology that has already contributed to theological interpretations that some view as aligning with current events in Gaza.

Before we proceed, let me be clear: belief, any belief, no matter how radical, is not inherently a problem. Every person is entitled to believe in whatever gives them inner peace, spiritual clarity, or moral direction. Faith is deeply personal, and its diversity is part of our shared humanity.

However, a belief becomes a problem when it manifests as actions that infringe on the rights, dignity, or lives of others. When theology becomes a justification for violence, displacement, or silence in the face of suffering, it ceases to be a private conviction and becomes a public threat.

This book does not challenge belief, it challenges the consequences of belief when weaponized against others.

## Anti-Human Theology: Empathy as Heresy

Certain interpretations within **Christian Zionism** have been critiqued as fostering views that may unintentionally **dehumanize others**. It reduces global suffering to **prophetic necessity**. It sanctifies **war, displacement, and injustice** as divine milestones. In this framework, compassion becomes heresy. It teaches millions that empathy is a threat to faith, and that compassion must be suspended when prophecy is in motion.

This theology has created a moral firewall around Israel. The suffering of Palestinians is not ignored out of cruelty, it is ignored out of theological obligation. To empathize with the oppressed is to question God's plan. To advocate for peace is to delay the Second Coming.

This is not religion. It is prophetic misapplication and theological distortion of the teachings of Jesus.

Some interpretations within Christian Zionism suggest that global conflict is a necessary precursor to redemption. It glorifies destruction as divine choreography. It welcomes chaos, war, and death, not as tragedies to be prevented, but as signs of progress. It is a theology that celebrates the end of humanity as the beginning of salvation.

It's important to mention that Islam, so often demonized in the media as violent, has nothing in its doctrine that compares to the scale, ambition, and cruelty of Christian Zionism. No other modern belief system has fused religion, empire, and end-times warfare so completely. No other ideology has turned empathy into heresy and conquest into worship.

While Islam, like all major religions, has been misused by political actors, its core teachings emphasize mercy, justice, and the sanctity of life. The Qur'an repeatedly calls for compassion toward the oppressed, the orphan, and the stranger. In contrast, Christian Zionism is not merely a distortion of Christianity, it is a theological inversion. It sanctifies suffering, glorifies war, and frames genocide as divine fulfillment. It does not call for peace, it demands apocalypse.

This is not a fringe belief. It is a mainstream theology that has shaped U.S. foreign policy, justified military aggression, and silenced empathy for millions of Palestinians. It is a belief system that teaches its followers to cheer for the collapse of the world, to see human suffering as a sign of spiritual progress, and to view justice as a threat to prophecy.

In this light, Christian Zionism, as a theological-political ideology, can lead to outcomes that contradict the ethical teachings of Christianity and the shared values of humanity. It is a theology that has replaced the Sermon on the Mount with the Book of Revelation, and the call to love one's neighbor with a mandate to dominate them. It is not a faith, it is a formula for annihilation.

This chapter is not a warning. It is a reckoning. And it begins by turning to face the ideological engine in full daylight.

## The Switch in the Mind: A Manufactured Reflex

In the introduction to this book, I described a recurring experience, what I called the "switch in the mind." It was the moment when empathy vanished. When a well-meaning American Christian, moved by the story of Palestinian suffering, suddenly shut down. The moment Israel was mentioned, something changed. A mental barrier rose. The suffering of Palestinians became irrelevant, even justified. The conversation ended.

This **switch** is not psychological alone, it is **theological**. It is the result of **decades of conditioning through sermons, media, and scripture annotations**. It is powered by dispensationalist theology, which teaches that history is unfolding according to a divine script, and that Israel must be supported at all costs, even if that cost is human life.

## Antisemitism Disguised as Support

Christian Zionism claims to support the Jewish people. But its support is conditional, instrumental, and ultimately destructive. According to dispensationalist doctrine, Jews must return to Palestine, rebuild the Temple, and accept Jesus as the Messiah, or face annihilation in the final battle of Armageddon.

This is not solidarity. It is spiritual coercion.

The Scofield Reference Bible embedded this theology into scripture, teaching generations of American Christians that Jews are pawns in a divine drama, not partners in faith, not equals in humanity, but instruments of prophecy. The theology does not celebrate Jewish survival, it anticipates Jewish death.

It does not honor Jewish identity, it seeks its erasure through conversion or destruction.

Christian Zionism is antisemitic not in spite of its support for Israel, but because of it.

While dispensationalist theology anticipates a violent eschatological outcome for Jews who do not convert, it is essential to recognize that not all Christian Zionists subscribe to this vision, nor are they fully aware of it. Many Christians support Israel out of genuine empathy for the Jewish people, especially in light of the Holocaust and centuries of persecution in Europe. Their support is often rooted in moral solidarity rather than theological strategy (Ariel, 2013; Spector, 2009).

Furthermore, most Christian Zionists who believe the phrase "God will bless those who bless Israel" applies to the modern state of Israel are not deeply versed in the theological framework of dispensationalism. They are unaware that their beliefs, if taken to their theological conclusion, anticipate the annihilation of (Israel) Jews who do not convert and the rest of humanity. These individuals are not malicious. They are misinformed. Their support is sincere, but the theological implications are obscured by decades of cultural reinforcement and selective teaching (Weber, 2004; Pew Research Center, 2005).

## Self-Fulfilling Prophecy: The 1948 and 1967 Wars

Christian Zionists frequently cite the **establishment of the State of Israel in 1948** and its **territorial expansion during the Six-Day War in 1967** as incontrovertible evidence of **biblical prophecy fulfilled**. These events are celebrated in sermons, literature, and political discourse as divine milestones, proof that God's eschatological plan is unfolding and that Israel's victories are sacred (Sizer, 2004; Mangum & Sweetnam, 2009). Yet this interpretation is not only theologically problematic; it is historically misleading.

The founding of Israel and its subsequent military triumphs were not spontaneous acts of divine intervention. They were the result of deliberate political maneuvering, diplomatic agreements, and military strategy, often executed with full awareness of their theological implications (Fromkin, 1989; Laqueur, 2003). More critically, these developments were shaped by a theological framework that had already declared what must happen for prophecy to be "fulfilled." In other words, they were self-fulfilling prophecies: events engineered to conform to a prewritten eschatological script.

Dispensationalist theology, formulated by John Nelson Darby in the 19th century and popularized through the Scofield Reference Bible in the early 20th century, provided this script. It outlined a prophetic roadmap that included the restoration of Jews to Palestine, the rebuilding of the Temple, and the rise of the Antichrist (Blaising & Bock, 1993; Mangum & Sweetnam, 2009). These steps were not presented as passive predictions but as imperatives, tasks that believers were called to advance. Christian Zionists embraced this mandate, transforming prophecy into policy and theology into geopolitical strategy.

Stephen Sizer's seminal work, *Christian Zionism: Road-map to Armageddon?*, underscores this dynamic, arguing that dispensationalism reimagined scripture as a political blueprint rather than a spiritual guide (Sizer, 2004). By embedding eschatology into foreign policy, Christian Zionism sanctified territorial expansion and normalized the dispossession of Palestinians as a divine necessity.

The Scofield Reference Bible institutionalized this worldview by integrating dispensationalist commentary into the biblical text, teaching generations of American Christians that supporting Israel was not merely a political preference but a spiritual obligation (Mangum & Sweetnam, 2009).

When Israel declared independence in 1948, Christian Zionists interpreted the event through Ezekiel 36–37; when it captured East Jerusalem and other territories in 1967, they invoked Zechariah 12. These interpretations framed geopolitical realities as sacred inevitabilities, absolving adherents of moral responsibility for their human cost. The displacement of Palestinians, the destruction of homes, and the denial of basic rights were not seen as injustices, they were reframed as prophetic milestones (Weber, 2004).

This theological posture is profoundly dangerous. It erases historical complexity, silences ethical accountability, and transforms empathy into heresy. By casting war and occupation as divine choreography, Christian Zionism legitimizes violence and undermines efforts for peace. It is not religion in its authentic sense; it is theological imperialism, a system that weaponizes faith to justify conquest and perpetuate suffering.

The 1948 and 1967 wars were not divine interventions. They were human decisions, executed within a framework that conflated prophecy with policy and scripture with statecraft. Recognizing this reality is essential, not only for historical accuracy but for moral clarity. Until this theology is confronted, the cycle of self-fulfilling prophecy will continue to shape geopolitics, sanctify injustice, and obstruct the pursuit of peace.

## From Kampala to The Hague: Christian Zionism's Global Reach

While Christian Zionism is often framed as an American phenomenon, rooted in Southern evangelicalism and shaped by figures like Falwell, Hagee, and Robertson, it is increasingly clear that its influence is global. One of the most striking examples of this international reach is the case of Judge Julia Sebutinde, a Ugandan jurist serving on the International Court of Justice (ICJ).

In 2024, the ICJ issued a series of rulings in response to South Africa's case against Israel, accusing it of genocide in Gaza. These rulings included provisional measures ordering Israel to prevent genocidal acts, allow humanitarian aid, and report back to the court. Over the course of six major decisions, the court overwhelmingly sided with South Africa's claims and issued binding orders to Israel. The votes were not unanimous, but they were decisive.

Judge Julia Sebutinde was the only judge to consistently vote against all six provisional measures. Her dissenting opinions rejected the court's findings of plausibility regarding genocidal intent and dismissed the urgency of humanitarian intervention. Her legal reasoning was widely criticized for aligning more with political apologetics than judicial neutrality. What made her voting pattern particularly controversial was not just its legal divergence, but its theological underpinning.

Sebutinde is publicly affiliated with the Watoto Church, a prominent evangelical megachurch headquartered in Kampala, Uganda. Founded in 1984 by Canadian missionaries Gary and Marilyn Skinner, Watoto began as a small congregation. Its name, "Watoto," meaning "children" in Swahili, reflects its early mission to care for orphans and vulnerable children, particularly those affected by Uganda's civil war and HIV/AIDS epidemic. Over time, it evolved into a full-fledged megachurch with a strong emphasis on prosperity theology, charismatic worship, and global outreach. Central to its doctrine is a deep commitment to Christian Zionism.

Watoto teaches that supporting Israel is a biblical mandate. Its sermons, prayer events, and fundraising campaigns frequently cite Genesis 12:3, "I will bless those who bless you", as justification for unwavering support. In 2023, the church launched a campaign titled "Bless Israel," encouraging congregants to donate to Israeli causes. Despite Uganda being one of the poorest countries in the world, with over 40% of its population living in poverty, Watoto and other Ugandan churches send substantial donations to Israel.

This phenomenon, churches in impoverished nations sending money to a wealthy, militarized state, highlights the theological inversion at the heart of Christian Zionism. It is not driven by humanitarian concern or economic logic. It is driven by eschatology. The belief that Israel must be supported at all costs, regardless of its actions or the donor's circumstances, is sanctified in pulpits and codified in doctrine.

These funds support Israeli charities, settlement infrastructure, and temple-related organizations such as the Temple Institute in Jerusalem. Once again, the donations are framed not as charity, but as prophecy fulfillment.

In public remarks following the ICJ proceedings, Sebutinde declared, "I am standing with Israel because the Lord has called me to do so." She added, "This is not just a legal matter, it is a spiritual one. I believe the Lord wants me to stand with His people." These statements sparked international debate. Legal scholars questioned whether theological convictions should influence judicial decisions at the world's highest court. Human rights advocates expressed concern that religious ideology was being used to justify impunity. And theologians pointed to Sebutinde's statements as evidence of the global spread of Christian Zionism, a movement that now shapes not only foreign policy, but international law.

Even more striking was the presence of an Israeli judge on the ICJ bench: Aharon Barak, a former President of Israel's Supreme Court. Barak recused himself from some votes but participated in others. His rulings were predictably favorable to Israel, but even he did not oppose all six provisional measures. In fact, Barak abstained or voted with the majority on certain humanitarian provisions, acknowledging the severity of the crisis. In contrast, Sebutinde's blanket opposition to every measure made her stance more extreme than that of Israel's own representative.

This juxtaposition, between a Ugandan judge influenced by Christian Zionist theology and an Israeli judge navigating legal diplomacy, underscores the paradox of Christian Zionism. It is often more zealous, more absolutist, and more resistant to compromise than Jewish Zionism itself.

The case of Judge Sebutinde illustrates a critical point: Christian Zionism is not confined to the Bible Belt. It is not limited to televangelists or American politicians. It is a transnational theology that has penetrated legal institutions, political systems, and religious communities across continents. From Kampala to The Hague, the belief that Israel must be defended at all costs is being sanctified in churches and codified in international law.

This global expansion of Christian Zionism poses a profound challenge to international justice. When judges see themselves as agents of prophecy rather than interpreters of law, the very foundation of legal neutrality is undermined. And when theology overrides evidence, the victims of violence are not just denied justice, they are erased from moral consideration.

Christian Zionism is no longer just a theological movement. It is a global ideology with legal, political, and humanitarian consequences. And unless it is confronted, not just in churches, but in courts, it will continue to sanctify suffering and silence accountability.

## Arguments for Confrontation

To dismantle Christian Zionism, we must formulate arguments that are theological, ethical, historical, and political. Here are the most effective ones:

### 1. Theological Argument: God Favors Israel Above All

- **Christian Zionist Claim:** God made an eternal covenant with the Jewish people and the land of Israel. Supporting modern Israel is not optional, it is a divine command. To bless Israel is to align with God's will; to oppose it is to invite judgment (Genesis 12:3).

- **Counterpoint:** This interpretation reduces God to a nationalist deity, more concerned with real estate than righteousness. It contradicts the universal message of Christianity, which teaches that God's love transcends borders, ethnicities, and nations. Jesus preached compassion for all people, including enemies (Matthew 5:44), not blind allegiance to a single state.

- **Why It Matters:** By turning God into a land broker and prophecy into policy, Christian Zionism distorts the gospel into a geopolitical agenda. It replaces the call to love one's neighbor with a mandate to defend a nation-state, regardless of its actions.

## 2. Ethical Argument: Compassion Must Yield to Prophecy

- **Christian Zionist Claim:** The suffering of Palestinians is unfortunate but necessary. It is part of God's prophetic timeline. Human empathy must not interfere with divine destiny.

- **Counterpoint:** This belief system turns compassion into disobedience. Yet scripture commands believers to "act justly, love mercy, and walk humbly with your God" (Micah 6:8). Jesus consistently sided with the oppressed and condemned religious hypocrisy (Matthew 23:23). Ignoring suffering in the name of prophecy is a betrayal of the gospel's moral core.

- **Why It Matters:** When empathy is framed as a threat to faith, injustice becomes invisible. This theology numbs the conscience, enabling complicity in war, occupation, and ethnic cleansing under the guise of obedience to God.

## 3. Historical Argument: Modern Israel Is the Fulfillment of Prophecy

- **Christian Zionist Claim:** The founding of Israel in 1948 and its military victories in 1967 are proof that biblical prophecy is being fulfilled. These events validate the Bible and confirm God's hand in history.

- **Counterpoint:** These were political and military events shaped by colonialism, diplomacy, and armed conflict, not divine intervention. Jesus warned against obsessing over signs and dates (Matthew 24:36) and emphasized the kingdom of God as a spiritual reality, not a geopolitical one (Luke 17:20–21).

- **Why It Matters:** When history is interpreted through a prophetic lens, it becomes a script to be followed rather than a reality to be shaped. This mindset justifies violence and territorial expansion as sacred, erasing the human cost of these policies.

## 4. Political Argument: Theology Should Shape Foreign Policy

- **Christian Zionist Claim:** U.S. foreign policy must align with biblical prophecy. Supporting Israel ensures national blessing; pressuring Israel invites divine punishment.

- **Counterpoint:** Jesus taught that his kingdom is "not of this world" (John 18:36). The early church rejected the fusion of faith and empire. When theology dictates foreign policy, it replaces diplomacy with dogma and undermines democratic principles rooted in justice and human rights (Proverbs 21:3).

- **Why It Matters:** When religious ideology drives international relations, it leads to endless conflict. It prevents peace, fuels extremism, and turns sacred texts into tools of statecraft.

## 5. Interfaith Argument: Christian Zionism Honors the Jewish People

- **Christian Zionist Claim:** Christian Zionism is an expression of love and solidarity with Jews. It supports their return to the Holy Land and protects them from antisemitism.

- **Counterpoint:** This "support" is conditional and instrumental. Christian Zionism envisions a future where Jews must convert or perish (Revelation 19:11–21). True love does not manipulate others for theological ends. Paul teaches that love "does not dishonor others... it always protects" (1 Corinthians 13:4–7).

- **Why It Matters**: Christian Zionism's version of "support" can have antisemitic consequences. It often treats Jewish identity as instrumental to a prophetic narrative, rather than honoring it as sacred and autonomous. I do not speak as a theologian, but as someone who has seen how this framing can erase both Jewish and Palestinian humanity.

Palestinian Christians are often marginalized by their Western evangelical brethren. Leaders such as Naim Ateek and Mitri Raheb have long criticized Christian Zionism as a theology that ignores justice and erases the lived experience of indigenous Christians in the Holy Land. In 2009, a coalition of Palestinian Christian leaders issued the Kairos Palestine document, which condemned Christian Zionism as a "false theology" that legitimizes oppression and violates the teachings of Christ (Kairos Palestine, 2009).

As Naim Ateek wrote, "Christian Zionism is a political movement that has nothing to do with the teachings of Jesus Christ. It is a movement that supports the occupation and denies justice." Mitri Raheb added, "We are the living stones of the land where Christianity was born, yet our voices are silenced by those who claim to speak for us."

Including these voices is essential, not only to challenge theological distortion but to restore the humanity of those most affected. Palestinian Christians and Muslims alike describe the experience of facing an alliance of foreign religious zealotry that supports their dispossession. Their testimony reframes the "war on Palestine" not as abstract theology, but as lived trauma.

## 6. Humanitarian Argument: Prophetic Ends Justify Catastrophic Means

- **Christian Zionist Claim:** The end-times must unfold as written. War, chaos, and mass death are necessary steps toward Christ's return. These events are not to be prevented, they are to be welcomed.

- **Counterpoint:** Jesus wept over Jerusalem and longed for peace, not destruction (Luke 19:41–42). The Bible calls believers to be peacemakers (Matthew 5:9), not cheerleaders for catastrophe. Any theology that anticipates or celebrates mass death is a perversion of the gospel.

- **Why It Matters:** This belief system sanctifies violence and undermines efforts for peace. It turns genocide into gospel and makes human suffering a sign of spiritual progress. No theology that justifies annihilation can claim moral authority.

While Christian Zionism has played a central role in shaping support for Israel's policies, it is important to recognize that not all Jews subscribe to Jewish Zionism or endorse the actions of the Israeli state. Throughout history, and especially in recent years, many Jewish voices have spoken out against the occupation of Palestine and the atrocities committed in their name. These voices, once marginalized and rarely heard, have grown louder and more organized, particularly in response to the war on Gaza and the genocide that followed. Jewish activists, scholars, and faith leaders have mobilized in solidarity with Palestinians, forming organizations that advocate for justice, human rights, and the establishment of a free Palestinian state. Their resistance challenges the notion that Zionism represents all Jews and affirms that moral conscience transcends religious identity. Including these voices is essential, not only to confront theological distortion but to restore the integrity of interfaith solidarity and the universal pursuit of justice.

Many Jewish voices have also spoken out against Zionism and Christian Zionism, challenging the notion that these ideologies represent all Jews. Organizations such as **Jewish Voice for Peace**, **IfNotNow**, and **Neturei Karta** have consistently opposed the occupation of Palestine and the theological narratives that justify it. Their resistance affirms that moral conscience transcends religious identity and that solidarity with Palestinians is not limited to any one faith tradition.

As **Jewish Voice for Peace** states: "*We oppose Zionism because it is a political ideology that has resulted in the displacement and oppression of Palestinians. Our Judaism calls us to pursue justice, not supremacy.*"

Similarly, **Neturei Karta**, an Orthodox Jewish group, has long maintained that "*Zionism is a rebellion against God. The Jewish people are forbidden to have their own state before the coming of the Messiah.*"

These voices remind us that the struggle for justice is not a religious conflict, it is a human one. Including Jewish dissenters not only challenges theological distortion but restores the integrity of interfaith solidarity.

## How to Confront It

Confrontation must be strategic, compassionate, and relentless. Here's how:

- Educate: Teach the history of dispensationalism and its political consequences.
- Expose: Reveal the manmade origins of prophecy, Darby, Scofield, and their theological inventions.
- Engage: Speak to Christian audiences with respect, but challenge their assumptions.
- Amplify: Support voices, Christian, Jewish, Muslim, and secular, that advocate for justice and peace.
- Reframe: Replace apocalyptic narratives with ethical theology rooted in compassion, justice, and coexistence.

## Conclusion: Turning Off the Switch

The switch in the mind is not permanent. It can be turned off. But only if we confront the theology that powers it. Christian Zionism is not just a belief, it is a system of influence. I do not claim theological authority, but I have witnessed how this ideology can suppress empathy and justify suffering. This book is not a critique of faith, it is a call to examine how belief, when politicized, can be used to silence compassion.

To dismantle it, we must speak truth, boldly, clearly, and persistently. We must remind the world that prophecy is not destiny. That theology must never override humanity. And that the true measure of faith is not how well we fulfill scripture, but how deeply we love our neighbor.

And there is hope. Recent polling indicates that younger evangelicals are increasingly questioning the theological and political assumptions of their elders. A 2021 Lifeway Research study found that only **33% of evangelicals aged 18–29** said they supported Israel "no matter what," compared to **62% of those aged 65 and older** (Lifeway Research, 2021). This generational divide has continued to widen. A 2023 survey by the **University of North Carolina and Lifeway Research** reported that support for unconditional backing of Israel among evangelicals under 30 dropped further to **28%**, while older cohorts remained largely unchanged (UNC & Lifeway Research, 2023). Similarly, a **2024 Pew Research Center poll** revealed that **younger evangelicals are twice as likely as older ones to favor conditioning U.S. aid to Israel on human rights compliance**, signaling a significant shift toward ethical accountability (Pew Research Center, 2024). These trends suggest that the once-monolithic evangelical support for Israel may be fracturing. The future of Christian theology may yet be reclaimed, not through prophecy, but through empathy.

# Final Call:
## The Switch Is Yours to Flip

I began this journey as a **young Palestinian student in the American South**, where the word **"Palestine"** was met not with recognition, but **confusion**.

*"Pakistinian?"* they'd ask.

*"No,"* I'd reply. *"Palestinian. From Palestine."*

And almost always, the conversation would end there.

**Palestine was invisible. Erased. Forgotten.**

But today, **everything has changed**.

The **genocide in Gaza** has shattered the silence.

The **ethnic cleansing of Palestine** has pierced the global conscience. **Now, the world knows.**

**Now, the world sees.**

**Now, the world must choose.**

This book is not just a chronicle of theology and politics. It is a reflection, an attempt to understand how belief systems shape conscience, policy, and perception.

**It is a call to awareness, not allegiance.**

The switch in the mind, the one that shuts down empathy, that silences truth, that erases Palestine, is not permanent. It can be examined.

And now, it must be.

The sacrifices of Gaza must not be in vain.

The lives lost, the homes destroyed, the children buried beneath rubble, they demand more than mourning.

They demand action.

They demand clarity.

They demand courage.

In the past, Christian Zionism and the Israel lobby succeeded in distorting reality.

They erased Palestine from textbooks, headlines, sermons, and hearts.

They turned scripture into strategy and prophecy into policy. But now, the veil has lifted.

Now, the lines are clear.

History often presents us with difficult choices.

Between dignity and denial.

Between justice and justification.

Between empathy for the oppressed and indifference to their suffering. This book **invites readers to reflect on those choices, not to prescribe them.**

**You must choose.**

**And you must act.**

Seek the switches in your community, your church, your classroom, your newsroom, your dinner table.

Find the moments when empathy falters.

Find the reflex that shuts down compassion.

And flip it.

When I was asked, "Why do you hate the Jews?"

I should have answered:

"We don't hate Jews. We never have. For centuries, Jews lived among us, in our cities, our culture, our history. We welcomed them when they fled Europe during the Holocaust. We opened our homes. We embraced them as equals.

What we oppose is Zionism, especially the Jewish Zionist movement that piggybacked on Christian Zionism to push a supremacist ideology and justify our dispossession.

So let me ask you: **Why do you believe it's acceptable to annihilate anyone who doesn't share your theology? Do you truly believe this is what God wants? That salvation must be built on suffering? That prophecy must be fulfilled through genocide?** Because if your belief system demands our erasure to feel righteous, then maybe it's not our hatred you should be questioning, it's your own."

This is not just about Palestine. It is about reclaiming our shared humanity. It means refusing to let theology override morality. It means choosing love over land, truth over prophecy, and justice over silence.

So go. Reflect. Reconsider. Reframe.

Because the world doesn't change when we understand it.

It changes when we refuse to look away and start speaking truth. It changes when we decide that prophecy is not destiny, and that justice is not optional.

It changes when we turn the switch back on.

# Glossary of Terms

## Aliyah
The immigration of Jews to Israel, often framed as a religious or prophetic return to the biblical homeland.

## Antichrist
A figure in Christian prophecy believed to deceive humanity before the return of Jesus. Often associated with global leadership and false peace.

## Apocalyptic Theology
A belief system focused on the end of the world, divine judgment, and the return of Christ. Often includes dramatic interpretations of biblical prophecy.

## Apostolic Tradition
Teachings and practices believed to have been passed down from the apostles of Jesus through successive generations of church leaders. It forms the foundation of doctrine in Orthodox and Catholic Christianity.

## Apostolic Succession
The belief that Christian authority is passed down through a continuous line of bishops dating back to the apostles of Jesus. This concept is central to both Catholic and Orthodox traditions.

## Armageddon
The final battle between good and evil, described in the Book of Revelation. Christian Zionists often believe this will occur in Israel.

## Bible Belt
A region in the United States, primarily in the South and parts of the Midwest, where evangelical Christianity is culturally dominant. The term refers to areas with high church attendance, strong conservative religious values, and significant influence of Christian beliefs on politics and education. The Bible Belt is often associated with widespread support for Christian Zionism and literal interpretations of scripture.

## Biblical Literalism
The interpretation of the Bible as a literal and factual account of history and prophecy, rather than symbolic or metaphorical.

## Bishop of Rome
The title held by the Pope, the leader of the Roman Catholic Church. The Bishop of Rome is considered the spiritual successor to Saint Peter, one of Jesus' apostles.

## Canon / Canonization (of Scripture)
The process by which certain books were officially recognized as part of the Bible. The "canon" refers to the accepted list of sacred texts.

## Church Age
In dispensationalist theology, the current era between Christ's resurrection and the Rapture, characterized by grace and evangelism.

## Clergy
Ordained leaders within the Christian Church, such as priests, bishops, and deacons, who are responsible for conducting religious services and guiding the spiritual life of the community.

## Conciliar Model
A form of church governance in which decisions are made collectively by councils of bishops rather than by a single central authority like the Pope. This model is used in Orthodox Christianity.

## Council (Ecumenical Council)
A formal assembly of church leaders convened to discuss and decide on matters of doctrine, practice, and church governance. The First Council of Nicaea (325 CE) is one of the most significant.

## Council of Nicaea
A gathering of Christian bishops in 325 CE, called by Emperor Constantine, to unify Christian doctrine. It produced the Nicene Creed and helped define early Christian beliefs.

## CUFI (Christians United for Israel)
A major Christian Zionist organization in the U.S. that mobilizes evangelical support for Israel through lobbying and fundraising.

## Doctrinal Unity
Agreement among members of a religious group on core beliefs and teachings. In early Christianity, this was often enforced through councils and creeds.

## Eastern Orthodox Churches
Christian denominations that developed in Eastern Europe and the Middle East. They trace their origins to the earliest Christian communities and differ from the Roman Catholic Church in theology, liturgy, and leadership structure.

## Ecclesiastical
Relating to the Christian Church or its clergy. The term is often used to describe things associated with church organization, authority, or religious practices, for example, "ecclesiastical power" refers to the influence held by church leaders or institutions.

## Edict of Milan
A proclamation issued in 313 CE by Emperor Constantine that legalized Christianity in the Roman Empire and ended the persecution of Christians.

## End Times
The period leading up to the Second Coming of Christ, often involving global conflict, suffering, and divine judgment.

## Enlightenment
A European intellectual and cultural movement of the 17th and 18th centuries that emphasized reason, science, individual liberty, and skepticism of traditional authority, particularly that of the Church and monarchy. Often referred to as the "Age of Reason," the Enlightenment laid the groundwork for modern secularism, democratic governance, and scientific inquiry. In the context of this book, the Enlightenment is significant for its influence on Protestant eschatology and figures like Sir Isaac Newton, who applied rational analysis to biblical prophecy, blending scientific rigor with theological speculation.

## Eschatology
The study of the end of the world and final events in human history, including death, judgment, and the Second Coming.

## Evangelicalism
A branch of Protestant Christianity emphasizing personal conversion, biblical authority, and spreading the gospel.

## Fifth Monarchy Men
A radical Puritan sect active in 17th-century England during the Interregnum period. They believed in the imminent establishment of a divine kingdom on Earth, the "Fifth Monarchy", following the four historical empires described in the Book of Daniel (Babylonian, Persian, Greek, and Roman). The group sought to overthrow earthly governments to prepare for Christ's millennial reign and was known for its apocalyptic fervor and political activism.

## Freemasonry/Freemasons
A centuries-old fraternal organization known for its secretive rituals, hierarchical structure, and emphasis on moral philosophy, personal development, and mutual support. While not a religious group, Freemasonry incorporates symbolic language and allegorical teachings rooted in Enlightenment ideals and biblical imagery. In the context of this book, Freemasonry is referenced for its structural and cultural similarities to the Brethren Movement, particularly in its use of coded language, emphasis on hidden knowledge, and discreet influence across religious and political domains. Although the Brethren did not adopt Masonic rituals or symbols, their organizational style and long-term strategic vision have drawn scholarly comparisons to the Masonic ethos (Marsden, 1980).

## Haganah
A Jewish paramilitary group in British Mandate Palestine, later part of the Israeli military.

### Hierarchical Structure (Church)
An organizational system in which authority is ranked in levels, with the Pope or patriarch at the top, followed by bishops, priests, and deacons.

### Holocaust Legacy
The historical memory of the genocide of Jews during World War II, which influences Western support for Israel.

### IFCJ (International Fellowship of Christians and Jews)
An organization that channels evangelical donations to Israel for social programs, security, and immigration (aliyah).

### Indulgences
Certificates sold by the Catholic Church in the Middle Ages that claimed to reduce punishment for sins. The abuse of indulgences was a major cause of the Protestant Reformation.

### Israel (Modern State)
Established in 1948. Viewed by Christian Zionists as the fulfillment of biblical prophecy.

### Jerusalem Embassy Act
A U.S. law passed in 1995 calling for the relocation of the American embassy to Jerusalem, fulfilled in 2018.

### Jewish Zionism
A nationalist movement that emerged in the late 19th century among Jewish communities, advocating for the establishment of a Jewish homeland in Palestine. Jewish Zionism was initially a response to widespread antisemitism and persecution in Europe. Over time, it evolved into a political, settler-colonist project that led to the creation of the State of Israel in 1948. While its original aim was self-determination for Jews, its implementation has been associated with the displacement of Palestinians and ongoing conflict in the region.

### Kairos Palestine Document
A 2009 declaration by Palestinian Christian leaders condemning Christian Zionism as a theology that legitimizes oppression. A more recent document was released on November 14, 2025.

### Latin (as Church Language)
The official language of the Roman Catholic Church for centuries. Latin was used in scripture, liturgy, and theological writings, making religious texts inaccessible to most laypeople.

### Millennial Kingdom
A thousand-year reign of Christ on Earth, described in Revelation. Interpreted literally by dispensationalists.

## Mitri Raheb
A Palestinian Christian theologian who critiques Christian Zionism and advocates for justice and coexistence.

## Naim Ateek
Founder of Palestinian liberation theology. Known for challenging Christian Zionism and promoting justice for Palestinians.

## Palestinian Christians
Indigenous Christian communities in Palestine, often marginalized by Western evangelical narratives.

## Post-Millennialism
The belief that Christ will return after a long period of peace and righteousness on Earth, often brought about by the Church's influence.

## Pre-Millennialism
The belief that Christ will return before establishing a literal thousand-year reign on Earth. Central to dispensationalist theology.

## Pre-Tribulation
The belief that Christians will be taken to heaven (raptured) before a period of global suffering (Tribulation).

## Mid-Tribulation
The belief that the Rapture will occur halfway through the seven-year Tribulation period.

## Post-Tribulation
The belief that Christians will endure the entire Tribulation and be raptured afterward.

## Prophecy Fulfillment
The belief that current events, especially in Israel, are direct fulfillments of biblical prophecy.

## Rapture
The belief that true Christians will be taken to heaven before the Tribulation. A key event in dispensationalist theology.

## Reformation (Protestant Reformation)
A 16th-century religious movement that challenged the authority and practices of the Catholic Church, leading to the creation of Protestant denominations and the translation of the Bible into local languages.

## Replacement Theology
The belief that the Church has replaced Israel as God's chosen people. Rejected by dispensationalists and Christian Zionists.

## Revelation
The final book of the Christian Bible, also known as the Apocalypse. It contains symbolic and prophetic visions of the end times, including the return of Christ, the rise of the Antichrist, the battle of Armageddon, and the creation of a new heaven and earth. Revelation is central to dispensationalist and Christian Zionist theology, often interpreted literally as a roadmap for future global events.

## Roman Catholic Church
The largest Christian denomination, centered in Rome and led by the Pope. It developed as a centralized institution after Christianity became the official religion of the Roman Empire.

## Scofield Reference Bible
A Bible annotated by Cyrus Scofield that popularized dispensationalist theology in the U.S.

## Scripture
Sacred writings considered authoritative in a religious tradition. In Christianity, this refers to the Bible.

## Second Coming
The anticipated return of Jesus Christ to Earth, often linked to the restoration of Israel and global conflict.

## Temple Mount
A religious site in Jerusalem sacred to Jews, Christians, and Muslims. Christian Zionists advocate rebuilding the Jewish temple there.

## Theology
The study of the nature of God, religious beliefs, and the interpretation of sacred texts.

## Tribulation
A seven-year period of suffering and chaos following the Rapture, according to dispensationalist theology.

## Vulgate
The Latin translation of the Bible completed by St. Jerome in the late 4th century. It became the official version of the Bible used by the Catholic Church.

## West Bank
A territory occupied by Israel since 1967. Its annexation is supported by many Christian Zionists as part of prophecy fulfillment.

## Western Roman Empire
The western half of the Roman Empire, which collapsed in 476 CE. After its fall, the Catholic Church became the dominant institution in Europe.

## William Tyndale
An English scholar, priest, and linguist born in the late 15th century. Tyndale was the first to translate the Bible into English directly from Hebrew and Greek texts. His work laid the foundation for later English translations, including the King James Bible. He was executed for his efforts to make scripture accessible to the public.

## Zionism
A political movement advocating for the establishment and support of a Jewish homeland in Palestine.

# Bibliography

- Ariel, Y. (2013). *An unusual relationship: Evangelical Christians and Jews.* NYU Press.

- Ateek, N. S. (2017). *A Palestinian theology of liberation: The Bible, justice, and the Palestine–Israel conflict.* Orbis Books.

- Barak, A. (2024). *Separate opinions on Gaza proceedings.* International Court of Justice. Retrieved October 14, 2025, from https://www.icj-cij.org

- Blaising, C. A., & Bock, D. L. (1993). *Dispensationalism, Israel and the Church: The search for definition.* Zondervan.

- Brown, P. (1989). *The rise of Western Christendom: Triumph and diversity, A.D. 200–1000.* Blackwell.

- Catechism of the Catholic Church. (1997). *Part One: The Profession of Faith.* Vatican Publishing.

- Chomsky, N., & Herman, E. S. (1988). *Manufacturing consent: The political economy of the mass media.* Pantheon Books.

- Christians United for Israel. (2023). *About CUFI.* Retrieved October 14, 2025, from https://cufi.org

- Cohn, N. (1957). *The pursuit of the millennium: Revolutionary millenarians and mystical anarchists of the Middle Ages.* Oxford University Press.

- Daniell, D. (1994). *William Tyndale: A biography.* Yale University Press.

- Duffy, E. (1997). *Saints and sinners: A history of the popes.* Yale University Press.

- Eisenstein, E. L. (1980). *The printing press as an agent of change.* Cambridge University Press.

- Fromkin, D. (1989). *A peace to end all peace: The fall of the Ottoman Empire and the creation of the modern Middle East.* Holt.

- Hechler, W. H. (2009). *The Jerusalem bishopric.* Retrieved October 14, 2025, from https://books.google.com/books?id=wjc-AAAAYAAJ

- Herzl, T. (1988). *The Jewish state* (S. Avineri, Ed.). Dover Publications. (Original work published 1896)

- International Court of Justice. (2024). *Orders on provisional measures in South Africa v. Israel.* Retrieved October 14, 2025, from https://www.icj-cij.org

- Kairos Palestine. (2009). *A moment of truth: A word of faith, hope and love from the heart of Palestinian suffering.* Retrieved October 14, 2025, from https://www.kairospalestine.ps

- Kairos Palestine. (2025). *A moment of truth: A word of faith, hope and love from the heart of Palestinian suffering.* Retrieved December 3, 2025, from https://www.kairospalestine.ps

- Keynes, J. M. (1946). *Newton, the man.* In *Essays in biography.* Rupert Hart-Davis.

- Klinger, J. (2010, July). Reverend William H. Hechler—The Christian minister who legitimized Theodor Herzl. *Jewish Magazine.* Retrieved October 14, 2025, from https://www.israelanswers.com/sites/israelanswers.com/files/files/images/Hechler.pdf

- Kyle, R. G. (2012). *Apocalyptic fever: End-time prophecies in modern America.* Wipf and Stock Publishers.

- Laqueur, W. (2003). *A history of Zionism: From the French Revolution to the establishment of the State of Israel.* Schocken Books.

- Lifeway Research. (2021). *Evangelical attitudes toward Israel and the Israeli–Palestinian conflict.* University of North Carolina & Lifeway Research. Retrieved October 14, 2025, from https://lifewayresearch.com/2021/09/21/young-evangelicals-less-supportive-of-israel-than-older-generations/

- Lowenthal, M. (Ed.). (1978). *The diaries of Theodor Herzl.* Peter Smith Publishing.

- Luther, M. (1522/2005). *The New Testament: Translated by Martin Luther.* Fortress Press.

- MacCulloch, D. (2010). *Christianity: The first three thousand years.* Penguin Books.

- Mangum, D., & Sweetnam, M. (2009). *The Scofield Bible: Its history and impact on the evangelical church.* Tyndale House.

- Marsden, G. M. (1980). *Fundamentalism and American culture.* Oxford University Press.

- McDonald, L. M., & Sanders, J. A. (2002). *The canon debate.* Hendrickson Publishers.

- McGinn, B. (1998). *Visions of the end: Apocalyptic traditions in the Middle Ages.* Columbia University Press.

- Metzger, B. M. (1987). *The canon of the New Testament: Its origin, development, and significance.* Oxford University Press.

- Newton, I. (1991). *Observations upon the prophecies of Daniel and the Apocalypse of St. John.* Scholars Press. (Original work published 1733)

- Norton, D. (2000). *A textual history of the King James Bible.* Cambridge University Press.

- Patai, R. (1975). *The myth of the Jewish race.* Wayne State University Press.

- Pew Research Center. (2024). *Americans' views on U.S. aid to Israel and human rights conditions.* Retrieved October 14, 2025 from https://www.pewresearch.org/religion/2024/05/15/americans-views-on-israel-and-human-rights/

- Pew Research Center. (2005). *Evangelicals and Israel.* Retrieved October 14, 2025, from https://www.pewresearch.org/religion/2005/04/15/american-evangelicals-and-israel/

- Raheb, M. (2014). *Faith in the face of empire: The Bible through Palestinian eyes.* Orbis Books.

- ReliefWeb. (2025). *Gaza: A humanitarian foundation is a direct accomplice in Israel's killing and starvation machine and must be held accountable.* Retrieved October 14, 2025, from https://reliefweb.int/report/occupied-palestinian-territory/gaza-humanitarian-foundation-direct-accomplice-israels-killing-and-starvation-machine-must-be-held-accountable

- Ryrie, C. C. (1995). *Dispensationalism.* Moody Publishers.

- Sandeen, E. R. (1970). *The roots of fundamentalism: British and American millenarianism, 1800–1930.* University of Chicago Press.

- Sebutinde, J. (2024). *Public remarks following ICJ vote* [Video transcript]. Retrieved October 14, 2025, from international news archives.

- Sizer, S. (2004). *Christian Zionism: Road-map to Armageddon?* InterVarsity Press.

- Skinner, G., & Skinner, M. (2005). *Watoto: A story of hope.* Watoto Publishing.

- Spector, S. (2009). *Evangelicals and Israel: The story of American Christian Zionism.* Oxford University Press.

- Temple Institute. (2023). *Global donations report.* Retrieved October 14, 2025, from https://www.templeinstitute.org

- Uganda Bureau of Statistics. (2024). *National poverty report.* Retrieved October 14, 2025, from https://www.ubos.go.ug

- University of North Carolina & Lifeway Research. (2023). *Generational shifts in evangelical views on Israel.* Retrieved October 14, 2025 from https://lifewayresearch.com/reports/2023-generational-shifts-evangelicals-israel

- Watoto Church. (2023). *Bless Israel campaign.* Retrieved October 14, 2025, from https://www.watotochurch.com

- Weber, T. P. (2004). *On the road to Armageddon: How evangelicals became Israel's best friend.* Baker Academic.

# Image Credits

This book includes images sourced from public domain archives, Creative Commons repositories, and original photography. Every effort has been made to provide proper attribution where required.

## Public Domain Images

Images in the public domain are free to use without attribution, but we acknowledge their sources for transparency and reader reference:

- **Page 21:** *Martin Luther* – Public Domain, via Wikimedia Commons

- **Page 22:** *William Tyndale* – Public Domain, via Wikimedia Commons

- **Page 31:** *John Nelson Darby* – Public Domain, via Wikimedia Commons

- **Page 49:** Anthony Ashley Cooper, 7th Earl of Shaftesbury – Public Domain, via Wikimedia Commons

- **Page 50:** Henry John Temple, 3rd Viscount Palmerston – Public Domain, via Wikimedia Commons

- **Page 51:** Emily Mary Amelia née Lamb, Viscountess Palmerston – Public Domain, via Wikimedia Commons (cropped)

- **Page 51:** Arthur James Balfour – Public Domain, via Wikimedia Commons

- **Page 52:** David Lloyd George – Public Domain, via Wikimedia Commons

- **Page 52:** Orde Charles Wingate – Public Domain, via Wikimedia Commons

- **Page 57:** William Hechler – Public Domain, via Wikimedia Commons (cropped)

- **Page 57:** Friedrich I of Baden – Public Domain, via Wikimedia Commons

- **Page 57:** Kaiser Wilhelm II of Germany – Public Domain, via Wikimedia Commons

- **Page 58:** Theodor Herzl – Public Domain, via Wikimedia Commons

- **Page 59:** Alfred Dreyfus – Public Domain, via Wikimedia Commons

- **Page 64:** William E. Blackstone – Public Domain, via Wikimedia Commons

- **Page 71:** C. I. Scofield – Public Domain, via Wikimedia Commons

- **Page 80:** J. C. H. at Podium – Public Domain, via Wikimedia Commons (cropped)

- **Page 81:** Jerry Falwell – Public Domain, via Wikimedia Commons (cropped)

- **Page 81:** Pat Robertson – Public Domain, via Wikimedia Commons (cropped)

- **Page 88:** Harry S. Truman – Public Domain, via Wikimedia Commons

- **Page 88:** Ronald Reagan – Public Domain, via Wikimedia Commons (cropped)

- **Page 88:** George W. Bush – Public Domain, via Wikimedia Commons

- **Page 89:** Donald Trump – Public Domain, via Wikimedia Commons

- **Page 90:** Tucker Carlson – Public Domain, via Wikimedia Commons

- **Page 90:** Ted Cruz – Public Domain, via Wikimedia Commons